SH#T YOUR EGO SAYS

SH#T YOUR EGO SAYS

STRATEGIES TO OVERTHROW YOUR EGO
AND BECOME THE HERO OF YOUR STORY

James McCrae

HAY HOUSE, INC.
Carlsbad, California • New York City
London • Sydney • Johannesburg
Vancouver • New Delhi

Published and distributed in the United States by: Hay House, Inc.: www.hayhouse.com® • *Published and distributed in Australia by:* Hay House Australia Pty. Ltd.: www.hayhouse.com.au • *Published and distributed in the United Kingdom by:* Hay House UK, Ltd.: www .hayhouse.co.uk • *Published and distributed in the Republic of South Africa by:* Hay House SA (Pty), Ltd.: www.hayhouse.co.za • *Distributed in Canada by:* Raincoast Books: www.raincoast.com • *Published in India by:* Hay House Publishers India: www.hayhouse.co.in

Cover design: James McCrae • *Interior design:* Nick C. Welch • *Interior photos/illustrations:* James McCrae

Library of Congress Cataloging-in-Publication Data

Names: McCrae, James, date, author.
Title: Sh#t your ego says : strategies to overthrow your ego and become the hero of your story / James McCrae.
Other titles: Shit your ego says
Description: 1st edition. | Carlsbad, California : Hay House, [2017]
Identifiers: LCCN 2016037607 | ISBN 9781401951191 (tradepaper: alk. paper)
Subjects: LCSH: Conduct of life. | Ego (Psychology) | Peace of mind. | Self-realization.
Classification: LCC BF637.C5 .M3595 2017 | DDC 158.1--dc23
LC record available at https://lccn.loc.gov/2016037607

ISBN: 978-1-4019-5119-1

10 9 8 7 6 5 4 3 2 1
1st edition, February 2017

Printed in the United States of America

*Dedicated to my parents, my sisters,
and the light of inspiration,
which is everywhere.*

(And, I suppose, my Ego, a worthy opponent.)

CONTENTS

"Just as nature takes every obstacle, every impediment, and works around it—turns it to its purposes, incorporates it into itself—so, too, a rational being can turn each setback into raw material and use it to achieve its goal."
— *Marcus Aurelius*

Flamenco Beach, Culebra, November 2012

PART ONE

CULEBRA I:
THE SNAKE

Across the winding road of history, one of the most enduring mythological symbols, both ancient and modern, has been the snake. The snake metaphor has been used by cultures around the world to represent a spectrum of human experiences—good and evil, creativity and death, wisdom and temptation. In some Native American legends, for example, the snake is considered a living incarnation of Mother Earth who holds power over nature. When humankind respects nature, the legend goes, the snake respects mankind, and provides good weather and prosperity. When mankind disrespects nature, the snake disrespects mankind, sending drought and natural disasters. Vedic literature speaks of a powerful energy force, called kundalini, coiled like a snake at the base of the spine. They say that when we awaken this force through yoga and meditation, we will unlock higher levels of consciousness and creativity. Hinduism gives us Lord Vishnu, the great creator, who sat on a thousand-headed snake and exhaled a single breath that gave birth to the universe. In Haitian voodoo, the snake is a sacred symbol that personifies the bridge between physical and spiritual worlds. And, of course, we have the most famous snake of all. In Genesis, a snake appears to Eve in the Garden of Eden, tempting her with forbidden fruit. The snake promises knowledge and power, distracting Eve from her purpose and leading her—and, as the story goes, all of mankind—astray.

Culebra is a Spanish word that means snake. Culebra is also a small island 17 miles east of Puerto Rico. On this island, on the verge of a nervous breakdown, I hit rock bottom.

This book was an accident.

It was 10 o'clock in the morning, and the sun was already hot. Barefoot on Flamenco Beach, I checked my iPhone for messages. A few friends had texted to ask if everything was alright. I could not tell if everything was alright, so I put the phone back in my pocket and did not respond.

Culebra's defining characteristic is the white sand. It is both beautiful and strange and resembles sand in a state of shock. In *Moby-Dick*, Herman Melville wrote that the color white has an elusive quality which, when divorced from more kindly associations, could heighten the thought of terror. Melville cited the polar bear and the great white shark as examples. "What but their smooth, flaky whiteness makes them the transcendent horrors they are?" he questioned. To this list I would add the white sand of Flamenco Beach. The Atlantic Ocean was quiet and I was alone.

In the distance a red-tailed hawk darted from the trees and soared above the water. Had someone been watching, they would probably tell you that I looked cool and collected, like a monk watching the ocean tide come and go like a mantra. The view—lush green mountains, dark forests, a picturesque sun above the Caribbean Sea—was breathtaking, but inside I felt panic. The bright sun felt like an interrogation room. New York City was underwater, and I was homeless.

I didn't know what to do, so I sat on the beach and did nothing. One week earlier, Hurricane Sandy had ripped through New York City like a WeedWacker. It was measured as the worst storm in the city's history. Lower Manhattan was underwater, hundreds of people had died, and thousands more, including myself, had a fish tank for an apartment. *This is crazy*, I thought, taking a swig of red wine. It was too early to drink. I took another swig. I wanted to run away, to be somewhere else, but I looked around and there was nowhere to run. I closed my eyes and opened them again. The ocean remained but the hawk was gone.

"If you want to be a writer, you should move to New York City," everyone told me. So I did. I said good-bye to my career as an advertising executive, sold my possessions, bid adieu to my friends and family, and purchased a one-way ticket from Minneapolis–Saint Paul International Airport to LaGuardia Airport in Queens, New York. All I had to my name were a few suitcases and the vague recollection of something Paulo Coelho had written: "When you want something, all the universe conspires in helping you to achieve it." It seemed as though I had barely unpacked when the waves hit.

Hurricane Sandy's ferocity was unexpected. We knew a storm, some storm, was coming. But most people, including myself, took minor precautions. *Fuggedaboutit,* was our attitude. *This is New York. We don't run away from a little bad weather.* For reasons closer to boredom than safety, I spent the night of the storm in New Jersey with Madison, a girl I was newly dating. We matched our strong resolve with stronger drinks and spent the night watching movies one state away, safe from the storm. By 11 o'clock the electricity in Madison's apartment was blinking on and off, and the wind was blowing with intensity. We did not realize that a few miles away the Hudson River was rising, and Lower Manhattan was turning into a swimming pool. Madison's electricity went out, this time for good, so we went to bed. We made love on the fourth floor, then fell asleep as rain hit the windows. My new apartment in Broad Channel, Queens, however, located on the water in Jamaica Bay, was not so lucky. I had just signed the lease and was scheduled to move the next day. The water was knee-high before midnight. Within hours everything was destroyed.

I wanted to make a splash in New York City but this was not what I had in mind. The next morning, slightly hungover, I heard the news about my apartment. For the first time, the weight of jumping from my old life without a safety net hit me, and I felt helpless. *I gave up my career for this?* I thought. Already without a job, now I had nowhere to live. Taking inventory of my options, I decided that I could not move back to Minneapolis, not yet, not before I had accomplished anything. I entertained asking Madison if I could stay with her, but quickly dismissed the thought. After all, I barely knew her. I could have sent a mass Facebook message requesting an open couch or spare bedroom, but I was new to New York and had few close friends in the city. My mind was racing when my phone rang. It was my friend Jake. Like me, he had lost his apartment in the storm. Unlike me, he had a plan.

"Listen," Jake said. "I know what we can do. I have a friend who owns a cottage in the Caribbean. He's traveling and the cottage is empty. When the universe takes away your beach house, you know what they say? It's time to find a bigger beach. Are you in?"

I didn't give it a second thought. A few days later, Jake and I left the wreckage of New York City behind on a JetBlue flight to Puerto Rico. Upon arrival we put the last of our money together and bought tickets on a rusty two-passenger aircraft that carried us to Culebra, island of the snake.

Culebra possesses a beautiful silence that belongs to another world. Unlike the typical Caribbean tourist spot, you will not find luxury hotels and resorts spreading like bacteria around the ocean perimeter. Culebra (population 1,800) is small and unassuming. *Quaint* would be an appropriate adjective. The same could be said for the airplane that carried us to the island. It was a relic of a bygone era, similar to a wooden roller coaster being phased out of the carnival on account of excess rust and a tendency to screech while hurling terrified riders down its unpredictable arches.

After a rocky flight we landed, surprisingly, safely. We thanked the pilot in Spanish and walked away from the short runway into the dirt roads to look for our cottage. Chickens and lizards roamed the streets with the cocksure abandon of New York City cab drivers. It was nearing evening as we passed palm trees holding hammocks where sleeping locals soaked in the setting sun. We were among them and happy to be.

We arrived on election day, a Puerto Rican holiday. Walking past the island homes, we noticed homemade flags suspended on poles and draped from balconies. Posters with Spanish slogans and pictures of politicians with big grins were hanging on telephone poles and street signs. Voting was finished, and the celebration was beginning. We reached the cottage. Men sang in the distance while fireworks illuminated the sky. The entire island was pouring tequila and dancing to music blasting from truck radios. More than one gun was fired. I just wanted to sleep.

We stumbled into the cottage and I claimed the bigger bedroom. The bed was stiff and the window had no glass. Closing my eyes I heard music in the streets. I imagined that the island was celebrating my arrival. Soon that thought—and all others—evaporated into the humid air. I slept for 10 hours.

Boy meets Ego.

The next morning I woke up confused. *How did I get here?* I thought. The past week's activity was a blur—the hurricane, the flood, the airplane, the celebration—and as I traced my steps from Madison's comfortable bedroom to a stiff Culebra mattress, I suddenly felt alone. Wearing the clothes I had slept in—jeans and a T-shirt—I stood up and left the cottage. As I passed through the kitchen, I saw a bottle of red wine and took it with me.

I walked down the dirt road until I found a paved street and continued walking. I passed the chickens and lizards and continued walking. I passed men sleeping in hammocks and continued walking. I passed political posters and broken tequila bottles and leftover fireworks and continued walking. I continued walking for 45 minutes until I reached the ocean on the northern tip of the island, then I stopped.

I sat down in the sand and opened the wine. The sky was Dodger blue and the ocean stood resolutely calm. While I knew I was lucky to ride out the aftermath of the hurricane on a tropical island, I had just arrived in Culebra, I was worried about my future, and I already wanted to leave. *I'm a failure,* I thought. *I should never have moved to New York City. Why did I give up a good career and good apartment? I'm too old to be chasing my dreams.* I had believed that if I took a risk the universe would support me. Now I wasn't so sure.

As a kid, I wanted to be a writer above all else. Every night I looked outside my bedroom window and let my imagination wander away from my small Minnesota hometown. Before long, my imagination had outgrown my reality, and I wanted to expand my surroundings to give my dreams a bigger playground. My heroes had names like Whitman, Hemingway, García Márquez, Rimbaud, Blake, and Ginsberg. Writers, to me, were the last explorers. The four corners of the Earth had already been discovered, but writers explored a new frontier—the frontier of the mind.

From a young age, writing was my meditation. I remember turning off my thoughts so I could create space for words and sentences to flow effortlessly through me. Creativity is an act of listening. Before a writer can write, a writer must listen. When we listen closely, which anybody can do, we can hear inspiration singing in the space between our thoughts.

The art of listening was my first creative lesson. I kept my ears open, hoping to catch the sound of the muse as she flew past Minnesota on her way to another world. If I listened closely, I thought, maybe I could steal a good idea before anybody else could hear it. So I paid attention to the sound of silence, hoping to eavesdrop on some great cosmic secret. I knew that creativity was borrowed from a place beyond my logical mind.

Fast-forward 15 years. I was in my late 20s. My writing ambitions had been set aside, and my advertising career was picking up. I found myself playing the unfamiliar role of a fast-talking corporate professional. Driven and focused, I quickly rose through the ranks of the Minneapolis advertising industry. Writing was the last thing on my mind.

My days were packed with client presentations, creative brainstorms, more coffee than I could handle, and more meetings than I could count. My nights consisted of happy hours, hip-hop shows, nightclubs, more drugs than I wanted, and more girls than I can remember. I filled my apartment with things I did not need and spent my time with people I did not like. It was fun—for a while. But something elemental was missing. While alone, depression crept in. In my rush to get ahead I was compensating for something that was missing, something that I did not realize I had lost. I had forgotten the most important lesson of my childhood. I had forgotten how to listen.

On Flamenco Beach I reflected on the decisions that had led me to the island. I realized that I had spent the past decade chasing after society's definition of success, and in doing so I had become blind to my higher purpose, whatever it was or had been. Like so many others, I had valued success over purpose and acclaim over authenticity, and now there was nobody left to impress. The sun was bright but an inner shadow was cast over me. My thoughts pushed and pulled without resolution. It felt like I had been punched in the face. I wanted to be punched in the face. I wanted more wine. I wanted anything to distract me from my mind.

Where are these thoughts coming from? I asked myself. Surprised to discover such contempt within myself, I traced my thoughts back to their origin. *Why was I feeling insecure?* Because I was unemployed and homeless. *But why did I care?* I was worried that, without money or a job, I would never return to New York City. *But why did I care?* I was afraid that I had given up my career for a dream that would never come true. *But why did I care?* I was embarrassed to fail. *But why did I care?* I needed validation from others to compensate for my insecurities. *But why did I care?* Because I was unable to find happiness in the stillness of being. *But why did I care?* Because I felt I was lacking something. And since I was lacking, I was needy. I needed something, anything. I simply needed.

Bingo. I had discovered my Ego. And it had a lot of shit to say.

My Ego was the voice of dissatisfaction and attachment inside my mind. It had gone undetected for years, but it had always been there, influencing my decisions from behind the scenes. I had never before noticed my Ego because I had assumed that my Ego was the real me. But I am not my Ego. And you are not your Ego. We are not our thoughts. We are the consciousness below the surface of mental activity. The mind is like rippling water on the ocean surface. It changes unpredictably and swirls with the tide. The real me—and the real you—is the ocean from which these ripples arise. Our thoughts can be random and destructive, but our consciousness remains still and complete in spite of the turmoil happening on the surface.

We are not our thoughts. We are the consciousness
below the surface of mental activity. The mind
is like rippling water on the ocean surface.
It changes unpredictably and swirls with the tide.
The real me—and the real you—is the ocean
from which these ripples arise.

The Ego speaks from a mentality of lack and creates false narratives to justify this lack. "I need success. I need to impress people. I need attention." Sitting on Flamenco Beach, I realized that these narratives, however convincing an argument the Ego made, were not true. Our reality comes from the stories we tell ourselves. If I wanted to transform my life, I realized, I had to start telling myself a different story—a story that came from somewhere beyond my Ego.

Realizing that I was not my thoughts, I remembered something that I had forgotten for many years. I remembered to stop thinking and start listening. I paid attention to the space between my thoughts. At first it was not easy. Thoughts, both good and bad, were fighting for my attention—and the wine was still swirling in my brain—but the distractions of the outside world slowly faded as I turned my attention inward. What I discovered was a conflict raging inside myself.

This conflict inside myself, I realized, was the source of conflict outside myself. Two voices fought for my attention. The first voice was my Ego. It told me to be worried. Fixated on the past, it reminded me of my mistakes; fixated on the future, it gave me a million reasons to doubt the path ahead. The Ego was everywhere at once but never in the present moment.

I closed my eyes and focused on my breath. *Inhale. Exhale. Inhale. Exhale.* In the stillness of my mind I heard another voice. It was quiet, not nearly as loud as my Ego, but felt true. The voice told me to calm down, and reassured me that I was safe. "No matter how bad the moment appears, there is no reason to worry or run away." The air was warm but a cold shock ran through my body. "You are exactly where you need to be," my Higher Self said.

The voice was not only heard; it was also felt. It was intuitive, not mental. It was part of me but also beyond me. I could not comprehend where the voice came from, but I quieted my mind and continued to listen. All at once I realized that I was stranded on this island for a reason. Negative thoughts had been flying around my mind for as long as I could remember, and I had been following them blindly. Flamenco Beach was my dead end. Sitting alone on the white sand, I decided to have, for the first time in my life, an open conversation between my Ego and Higher Self.

My Ego said that I was a victim of circumstance.
My Higher Self said that I create my own reality.

My Ego told me to worry.
My Higher Self told me to trust the present moment.

My Ego said that everything was an accident.
My Higher Self said that everything had a purpose.

Find your ocean.

"When Ego is lost, limit is lost."

— YOGI BHAJAN

As a kid growing up in Minnesota, I had never seen the ocean. But near my home was a small pond that resembled a science project gone amok. Worms, tadpoles, frogs, and turtles roamed the exterior of the pond like guardians of a swampy kingdom. I remember pulling up my pants to wade in the water and feel mud squish between my toes. I had heard stories about giant bodies of water, far away, called oceans. But where were they? I had never seen them.

When we expand our capacity to perceive,
our capacity to experience also expands.
To be more, we must first imagine more.

On Culebra I realized that when we seek truth outside ourselves (in the form of success, media, politics, religion, and other types of social conditioning) we are wading in a small pond, a shallow version of what is possible. If we never see life from a broader perspective, we will always mistake the pond for the ocean. When our perception is limited, our reality is also limited. When we expand our capacity to perceive, our capacity to experience also expands. To be more, we must first imagine more.

We all have an ocean within us. This ocean is a state of being, not a place. It is energy, not water. When an actor gets lost in character, that is her ocean. When a father holds his newborn son for the first time, that is his ocean. When you fall in love and time stops, that is your ocean. You find your ocean by clearing your mind of distractions and accepting the moment as it is—both the beauty and the pain of life—without resistance.

Sooner or later we all find our ocean. This is inevitable because our ocean is our only destination. There is no failure, only progress. There is no fire, only water. All wrong turns reroute to the same holy highway. Some of us will find our ocean quickly. For others it will take a long time because we are afraid to venture away from the shore. Some will find our ocean because we are searching for it. For others, like me, it will be an accident. The Ego says that if we sail toward the ocean we will become lost at sea. It's not true. We will be sailing home.

Every stream reaches a river, all rivers reach the sea. When we flow with the present moment, we are guided by the wisdom of stillness. Even if you are stranded on an island you will not be homeless. You will be home. And your Ego will have nothing left to say.

Every beginning begins with an end.

Of all the metaphors represented by the snake, my favorite is rebirth. As the snake ages, its skin wears out and stretches, making it unable to support new growth. But the snake is not finished growing. It is still becoming the snake it wants to be. So the snake grows a new layer of skin under the old layer. When the new skin is ready, the snake sheds the old layer because it is no longer necessary. It holds no attachment or sentimentality to the identity it leaves behind.

Humans also shed our skin. Every day one million skin cells turn into dust and are replaced by new cells. Every seven years each cell in our body has died and been replaced. In a physical sense we become new people. All matter is alive, moving from state to state in varying degrees of change. We crawl, we walk, we run, we fly, we crash, and we rise again. We look back and see how our journey defined us. Along the way, part of us must die so that we can continue to grow. Shedding old cells is essential for the growth of our bodies, and shedding old ideas and beliefs is essential for the growth of our consciousness. This is the story of how, on the island of Culebra (the snake), I learned to shed the skin of my Ego—one idea, one belief at a time.

New York City, 2015

CHAPTER 1

WELCOME TO THE REAL WORLD

L ong ago, before time and space had taken shape, the Ego did not exist. Everything was one thing. All was empty and complete. There were no opinions, only imagination. There was no matter, only energy. From this stillness the universe took a deep breath and exhaled a single vibration that echoed across the canyons of nothing and over billions of years gradually expanded into something. The one thing became many things.

Long ago, before our capacity for doubt and attachment, our Egos did not exist. There was no judgment, only acceptance. There was no insecurity, only love. We had not yet made a distinction between ourselves and the ocean of consciousness from which we came. Our minds were diamonds. We were complete.

That was then. This is now.

"Complete? More like a complete idiot," my Ego said. "Look around. You are homeless. Look at your bank account. You are broke. Your entire life has been one mistake after another. I hate to break it to you, but there is no higher purpose guiding you. There is no treasure buried on this beach. You are a failure. Welcome to the real world."

Just because your mind says something does not make it true.

My head was spinning. Was it true? Had I been foolish to think that I could move to New York City without a plan and everything would magically be okay? Maybe the world was, like the perspective from a Bukowski poem, crueler than I wanted to believe.

Deep within my mind, closer to a feeling than a thought, I heard another voice.

"Just breathe," the voice said. "And allow the thoughts that do not serve you to fade away." It was my Higher Self. "Always remember that you are not your thoughts. You are the ocean of consciousness from which your thoughts arise. Don't identify with the waves. Be the ocean: still, unmoving. Just because your mind says something does not make it true. When you have a neutral mind—still during both good times and bad—and remain detached from the mood swings of your Ego, you will know which thoughts should be ignored and which deserve your focus. Otherwise your mind will behave like dust blowing in the wind, lost, with no foundation."

The waves came and went and for a moment it was beautiful.

What is the Ego?

In college I learned about the Freudian Ego. According to Freud's theories, the Ego is a fundamental aspect of human psychology. "The Ego represents what we call reason and sanity, in contrast to the id which contains the passions," Freud wrote in 1923. In other words, the Ego is the mind's police, keeping our animal instincts in check so we can operate as an organized society. The definitions of Freud, and later Carl Jung, satisfied me from an intellectual perspective, and I never thought any more about the Ego.

But the Ego I discovered on Culebra was different. It was self-deprecating, manipulative, and the source of pride, judgment, and limitation in my life. What is my Ego? Where did it come from? There are various opinions on what the word *ego* means. Science, psychology, and spirituality have all suggested various definitions. For the sake of this book I will add another. The Ego is *your reactive attached mind.*

- **Your:** Your Ego is yours alone. It does not exist to anyone other than yourself and has no authority beyond what you give it.

- **Reactive:** The Ego does not create. It only reacts. It could be described as the "reptilian brain," which by nature is reactive, territorial, defensive, and always in survival mode.

- **Attached:** The Ego clings to what is known. It is insecure and therefore unable to release attachment to past memories and future expectations. Attachment is the Ego's substitute for love.

- **Mind:** The Ego is a mental abstraction that believes nothing exists beyond its immediate perception and intelligence. "I think, therefore I am everything," it says. The Ego is logic drunk on power.

Freud was right. The Ego helps us manage our irrational behavior. It serves a useful purpose. And yet while the Ego suppresses our lower nature, it also suppresses our higher nature. It does not understand the difference. What Freud did not acknowledge was the Ego's tendency to hijack the ship of our consciousness and steer it blindly into the dangerous waters of worry, doubt, and limitation. The Ego makes a good shipmate, but is a terrible captain. The Ego sees the world from a limited perspective, and therefore has limited understanding. Following the Ego is like navigating a foreign city with a scrap from a torn-apart map.

On the eighth day, man created Ego.

Think back to your childhood. What was your attitude toward life? Children, unless they have experienced trauma, have a natural inclination to love others and themselves. They trust themselves and others because—not yet being capable of judgment or cynicism—trust is all they understand. A child uses her brain to make decisions, but she is guided by her heart. This is the state of being we are born into. But over time, little by little, we change. We gradually stop trusting ourselves and start conforming to the expectations around us. We stop living from the heart and begin living from the head. What happened? The Ego happened.

Our minds shifted gradually. It began the first time we felt separation or emotional pain. The world, it turned out, could be cruel and heartless, and this was a reality we were not prepared for. We felt a sudden need to protect ourselves. We began wearing masks. Our masks took the shape of emotional detachment and social conformity. We disguised ourselves because exposing our nature was too painful.

"Welcome to the real world," the Ego said. At first we didn't know if we should trust the Ego, so we asked for advice.

Everyone gave us the same answer: "Yes, this is the real world," they said. "I'm sorry, but it's true." Little by little, our friends started changing, so we changed too. And nobody could tell us why. We didn't find answers so we stopped asking questions. When we stopped asking questions, we stopped listening to the Higher Self. We drew a line in the sand between information and imagination, and stepped onto the side of information. We lost the ability to imagine, and therefore we lost our sense of purpose. It's not until years later, if ever, that we realize our mistake.

Free your thought.

"The commonsense rules of the 'real world' are a fragile collection of socially reinforced illusions."

— TIM FERRISS

Every society is built on commonly held agreements. For example, society has made an agreement to wear pants in public. We have agreed to use silverware when we eat and to respect personal space (this rule is optional on New York City subways). Most of these rules are, more or less, logical. They help us relate to each other and function as an organized community. But some agreements that society has made are less helpful, and sometimes even dangerous.

For example, society tells us that if we do not come from the right social class or attend the best university, too bad, we will never be successful. Society tells us that if we speak an unpopular truth, too bad, other people will reject us. Society tells us that if we challenge the status quo, too bad, we will fail. Social agreements such as these, even if well intended, serve to limit our potential. The beliefs we follow define our reality. Sunlight can only enter a window as much as the shades allow. Your life works the same way. When you narrow your beliefs, less light enters your window.

We live in two worlds. One is the eternal world of energy and vibration. Another name for this world, according to ancient Vedic texts, is Brahman. This is the world of imagination and the Higher Self. The other world is the temporary world of intelligence and materialism. Another name for this world, according to ancient Vedic texts, is Maya. This is the world of logic and Ego. These two worlds are in a constant balancing act. Sitting on the beach of Culebra, I witnessed a collision between them.

My Ego was fighting for my attention. "Don't waste your time with imagination and metaphysical thoughts," it said. "They are not real. Stop kidding yourself and admit that you are a failure. Life is hard. Accept it. This is the real world."

"Everything will be okay," my Higher Self reassured me. "Everything will always be okay. Your Ego is defensive because you are on the verge of discovering a world that is more real than its own. Your Ego is afraid, and is fighting for its life."

SH#T YOUR EGO SAYS

SH#T YOUR HIGHER SELF SAYS

EGO	#	HIGHER SELF
I am a victim of circumstance	①	I create my own reality
Uncertainty makes me afraid	②	Uncertainty makes me excited
I want to reach the status quo	③	I want to break the status quo
Life is random data	④	Life is creative energy
Happiness must be earned	⑤	Happiness is my birthright

CHAPTER 2

GET ME OUT OF HERE

The minute hand moved to 12 like a base runner sliding home. The hour hand pointed to nine as I looked at the clock with nervous attention. It was Monday morning and I already needed a break. It was week one at my new job—my dream job, I thought, as an advertising executive at a Minneapolis agency—and I was scheduled to meet my first client, a Fortune 500 retail company, in an hour. I already knew I was in trouble. The advertising business was not new to me. I had spent years working as a designer, and later a strategist, for clients in nearly every industry under the sun. But this job was different. I had jumped from the creative department to the account department. For the first time, I was given the keys to manage the timelines and budgets of global client accounts. To say I was afraid would be an exaggeration. To say I was confidant would be a bigger exaggeration.

Am I ready? I wondered. *Am I qualified?* I had been fired before and was afraid of it happening again. *Calm down,* I mentally responded. *Whatever you do, remember to breathe.* The worry did not go away completely. Walking into the client's 13th-floor office, I noticed I was holding my breath. I was also expecting failure. *Be careful what you expect,* I reminded myself. *You just might get it.*

The client team—high-ranking marketing executives—was waiting inside the conference room. I introduced myself. It was clear from the beginning—black suits, sharp eyes, handshakes that felt like competition—that this was a business with high expectations and low tolerance for mistakes. My job was to be diplomatic but inside I felt resistance. *I used to be creative, I thought. How did I end up here?* More than once I tried to lighten the mood with sarcastic humor. It was a technique that had worked well for me as a designer. Clients appreciate sarcasm and offbeat humor from the creative guys. Not so, it turned out, from the awkward executive leading the meeting in an uncomfortable gray suit. I felt the clients' eyes looking straight through me. Who they saw, I feared, was not a professional. He was an amateur.

No running allowed.

Time passed and the meeting ended. I made a few mistakes, rambled too much, but I survived, and it wasn't as bad as I feared. Things usually are not. My Ego, it turned out, had been telling me a story. It told me that I wasn't good enough, that I was in danger. This danger was not real. After all, it was just a meeting about advertising. But my Ego, acting defensively, was feeding me false information based in fear. Whenever the mind senses danger, it triggers our biological imperative to survive. For example, when facing a threat, humans have evolved the instinct to avoid danger by any means possible, compelling us to destroy any threat we face. And if the threat is too big to destroy, we do the next best thing. We run. This is known as the fight-or-flight response.

The path to insanity is believing false narratives. The path to wisdom is dropping fear based on what we believe, but do not know, to be true.

The fight-or-flight response has, over the course of human-kind, served a valuable purpose—especially in prehistoric times when we risked being eaten by tigers or beheaded by bad neighbors. But today, in many ways, our daily lives have evolved beyond our biological instincts. Most people (at least those of us lucky enough to be born into the first world) no longer face the same daily threats we faced in ancient or even feudal times. But our minds still react to conflict, even insignificant conflict, with the same heightened awareness. The downside here is that the fight-or-flight response can create fear and anxiety in situations that don't require either.

It is common for the modern person, including myself, to return home from work and, in spite of the fact that we are perfectly safe, experience intense feelings of worry and anxiety that can be traced to small moments of perceived threat that happened during the day. This anxiety manifests as fight-or-flight. If we choose fight, we become abusive to ourselves and others. If we choose flight, we grow absent and disconnected. These reactions often stem from an inaccurate interpretation of reality based on the Ego's limited perception. We perceive threats where none exist and run away from shadows.

Some threats are real. Things can go wrong. But it is important to ask ourselves whether our perception of danger is based on knowledge or assumptions. If our perception of danger is based on knowledge (such as the report of a hurricane), there is no need to dwell on fear because we have identified the problem and can take action toward a solution. And if our perception of danger is based on assumptions (such as the belief that people are judging us), there is also no need to dwell on fear because we do not have the facts to know for certain. The path to insanity is believing false narratives. The path to wisdom is dropping fear based on what we believe, but do not know, to be true.

Whenever I face perceived danger—hard jobs, for example, or relationship problems—my Ego tells me to run away. I become frustrated and want to escape my problems. For years, running away was my solution, and it got me nowhere. But when I observe problems in hindsight, I can see that they are not really problems. They are opportunities to grow. The irony is that when we avoid problems, we also avoid the solution. The solution is always found within the problem. The obstacle is the way.

Life changes when we do.

Every time we walk into a room, any room, we immediately experience a subjective reality. You and I could walk into the same room, and we each would perceive a different place. The setting would be the same. The same table, chairs, art, and people would greet us. But our attention would be drawn to different things. You might notice the conversation, and the style of the art on the walls. I might notice the smell of food cooking and the clothes people are wearing. If 100 people walk into the same room, there will be 100 different interpretations. Each interpretation is true but none is the entire truth.

Reality is a field of endless subjectivity. No human mind, however intelligent, can perceive it all. Everything that happens within the field of subjective reality is filtered through our individual perspective, resulting in our personal experiences. Your world is what you perceive, and my world is what I perceive. What separates your reality from mine? Our focus. The first step toward changing our lives, therefore, is changing our focus.

Running from problems is like running from a mirror because we don't like the unhappy face in the reflection.

When we focus on the stress of our job, our focus creates more stress. When we feel nervous in social situations and focus on this feeling, our attention causes our nerves to amplify the sensation. Whatever we place our attention on will manifest as our perceived reality. For this reason, worrying about a problem can never solve it, because worry gives attention to the problem—not the solution. But when we change our focus, we change our subjective reality, and our circumstances will eventually shift to reflect our new perspective.

Running from problems is like running from a mirror because we don't like the unhappy face in the reflection. We can run to a different mirror but will continue to see the same face until we stop running and choose to smile. The mirror changes when we do.

We all, at times, feel threatened by things beyond our control. But instead of reacting to fear by running away, we can use difficult moments to practice being fully present. When we are fully present, we can control our focus. When we control our focus, we control our reality. Acceptance of the moment, without running away or passing judgment, is the end of anxiety.

Fight-or-flight (or flow).

I returned to my office, poured a cup of coffee, and reflected on my fear of failing at my new job. I was surrounded by intelligent people and felt insecure. My Ego assumed that I was being judged, although I had no proof, and these assumptions caused me to worry. In truth, the only person judging me was myself.

Inhale. Exhale. Inhale. Exhale. "Instead of running away, try changing your focus," my Higher Self said. "Accept the present moment with a neutral mind. After all, good and bad are only ways of thinking." I still experienced doubt (and still do), but I realized that my doubt did not define me. When my job was easy, I stayed neutral. When I made mistakes, I stayed neutral. I stopped believing in the false narrative that had caused me to live in fear. Everything changed. Changing my focus changed my thoughts, and my job became easier as a result.

Fear is a great teacher because it allows us to practice courage. Having fear is normal. But having fear and focusing on fear are different things. When we remain neutral in the face of anxiety, we understand that fear is only a mirage. Any fool can run away. It takes courage to stand in our power.

CHAPTER 3

LIFE ISN'T FAIR

My career started slowly. In fact, it almost didn't start at all. Following high school, after a few years and more than a few wrong turns, I was searching for direction. So I enrolled in a private refuge for dreamers who, for as long as we could, refused to wake up—art school. I studied graphic design. We were taught the classics—Bauhaus, Modernism, Russian Constructivism—and were given assignments to translate those principles into various commercial media, such as advertisements, posters, websites, logos, and magazines. We were learning to bridge the gap between creativity and commerce.

After class I would walk to Barnes & Noble on Nicollet Mall in downtown Minneapolis and look at books by guys like Paul Rand, Milton Glaser, Tibor Kalman, Massimo Vignelli, and Stefan Sagmeister. They became my design heroes, and taught me the art of simplicity. Being a writer had already taught me the power of expression, and design school was teaching me the power of form. "There is no such thing as bad content, only bad form," Paul Rand said, and I believed him. Design is visual problem solving. Wisdom, I realized, can be found in the organization of things.

Everything has design—homes, cities, books, highway systems. Even intangible things, such as businesses or political systems, are designed by taking disconnected pieces and organizing them to serve a central purpose. "Good design is public service," one of my professors said, "because it makes the world work better. And the best design, because it works so well, goes unnoticed. It simply allows people to continue their day." Design school taught me to balance the right and left sides of my brain. Creativity for the sake of creativity was discouraged. The goal was creativity with purpose. We learned that stylistic bells and whistles actually interfere with the communication of a message. Good design includes exactly what is needed and nothing more.

Four years after starting design school I graduated at the top of my class. My life was falling into place, and I eagerly anticipated a career as a professional—maybe even famous— designer. All clear for takeoff and I had a first-class ticket. Then the recession hit.

The advertising industry, which employs many designers, thrives when the economy is good. But when corporations make cuts, their mentality shifts from growth to protection, and creativity is a luxury they can no longer afford. When the global economy collapsed in 2007, businesses everywhere, including advertising and design agencies, were making cuts, and there was a hiring freeze. This freeze was especially hard for young professionals because our limited experience made us expendable. Agencies stopped offering paid jobs to college graduates and instead offered unpaid internships. My classmates gladly accepted these unpaid internships. At least it was a foot in the door.

But I was already suffering from a personal economic recession. I was broke. No longer eligible for student loans, the clock was ticking on my rent and credit-card debt. I wanted to be a designer, but not as much as I wanted to eat. Many of my friends were financially supported by their families, so while they took unpaid internships that eventually led to high-paying jobs, I needed a paycheck right away, so I started working retail at Urban Outfitters.

After work I would meet my friends at our favorite bar near campus. Secretly jealous, I congratulated them on their success. I had believed that success resulted from talent and hard work, but everywhere I looked success was being defined by family connections and money. It was more than a reality check. It was checkmate. "I'm finished," my Ego said. "I can't compete with the benefits of privilege."

Expectation is the opposite of meditation.

You could be the most positive thinker in the world. You could have better karma than the Dalai Lama. It doesn't matter. We don't always get what we want.

This doesn't mean that life is unfair. Just because we want something does not mean the thing we want is best for us. We never know what the outcome of our circumstances will be, so it is foolish to make judgments about what is fair and unfair. Expectations are expensive. When we have expectations, our attention leaves the present moment and we exchange the power of now for the powerlessness of hope. The cost of this transaction is very high because we are trading what we can control (the present) for what we cannot control (the future). In doing so we accept lack as a reality because we have concluded that the present moment is not enough.

When we judge fairness by the satisfaction of the Ego, life can seem unfair. But the Ego, because it has limited perception, does not always understand what is best for us. Imagine a crying baby. The baby is crying because she wants more ice cream. In the baby's limited perception, it is unfair that she is not allowed to eat more ice cream. But the baby's parents have restricted her ice cream consumption because a balanced diet is healthier. There is purpose beyond the baby's capacity to understand. This is true for adults too. When circumstances seem unfair, there may be a purpose beyond the Ego's capacity to understand.

We don't always choose our circumstances. But we always choose how we react to our circumstances. When we resist the present moment, we struggle. When we trust the present moment, we flow. Difficult moments, when we embrace them, make us stronger. Pressure turns coal into a diamond, boot camp turns civilians into soldiers, and seemingly unfair circumstances can prepare us for a greater purpose.

Our imagination becomes our destiny.

Imagine something you want to happen. It could be a career, a relationship, more money, more creativity, anything. Hold this intention. Pause. Now quiet the mind. Imagine that what you want has already happened. See what it looks like. Hear what it sounds like. Feel what it feels like. Now examine your emotions. How do you feel? You probably feel good, but in what way exactly do you feel good? Are you excited? Relieved? Joyful? Now remember this—we receive from life the energy we project. When we feel the resulting emotion from our intentions now, before they have happened, we create the space within ourselves to achieve that specific result. We eventually become the person we imagine now.

Success doesn't happen by projecting expectations outward. It happens by cultivating presence inward.

Before we can *have*, we must *be*. Before we can *be*, we must *imagine*. When we think and feel lacking, we create more lack. When we think and feel complete, we create more completeness. Nothing happens in the future. Everything happens now. The next time you have a bad day, ask yourself—*Was I present?* The next time you fail to accomplish a goal, ask yourself—*Was I present?* The next time life seems unfair, ask yourself—*Am I being present?* We don't get what we want in life. We get who we are. Success doesn't happen by projecting expectations outward. It happens by cultivating presence inward.

Give up.

My Ego was angry that I worked retail while my friends became successful designers. By all accounts, I was lucky to be alive and have a steady paycheck, but my mind said that life was unfair because my job was not what I wanted or had chosen. Every day, while folding T-shirts and skinny jeans, I feared that I would never fulfill my personal expectations. Finally my frustration peaked, and I realized that I had two options: I could feel sorry for myself, or I could stop resisting and accept the possibility that an unseen purpose was guiding me. I took a deep breath and decided to accept—even trust—the present moment.

Acceptance gave way to opportunity. My manager at Urban Outfitters was married to an advertising art director, and one day she visited the store while I was eating lunch. I was in the break room showing my design portfolio to a co-worker (partially because my co-worker had asked, and partially because I desperately wanted people to know that I had talents beyond customer service).

My manager's wife overheard and asked if she could look. "Are you a designer?" she asked.

I passed my portfolio over the table. "Yes," I mumbled. "But I'm still looking for a job."

She silently reviewed my portfolio.

"You're good," she finally said. "You should e-mail me." She handed me a business card.

"Thanks," I muttered, and returned to work because my break was over.

E-mails were exchanged. Two weeks later she offered me a job—not an unpaid internship. I was blown away. The thing that I had perceived to be unfair, my job in retail, had quietly worked to create my greatest opportunity.

Yes, from the Ego's perspective, life can seem unfair, and it will break us down until we stop expecting to get exactly what we want. And that is the great "aha!" moment—when our Ego is broken down so much that we stop resisting the present moment and start trusting uncertainty. What the Ego considers unfair, we then realize, is part of a greater purpose.

Each person is an instrument within an orchestra. Our job is to play the notes assigned to the best of our ability. We might not enjoy every note, but life is not an individual performance. Every note makes sense in the context of the symphony. When we attempt to control the melody, we will be out of sync with the whole. Happiness cannot be acquired; happiness is reductive. It is all that remains when we strip away the Ego and see the universal harmony of which we are each a small, yet essential, instrument.

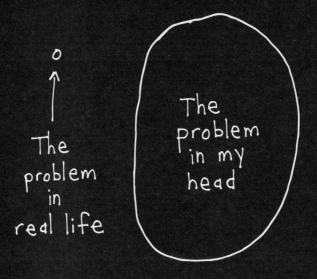

CHAPTER 4

ONLY RESULTS MATTER

Guys know what I'm talking about. There's nothing worse. I will never forget the first time it happened to me. Sometimes I remember and still feel embarrassed, although many years, and many girlfriends, have since passed. It happens to everyone, they say, but those words do not help. "It's no big deal," she says. "I still had a nice night." And she will kiss you, but the kiss will feel different from before, which might be real or it might be imagined, and it is not knowing that causes the most frustration.

It was June in Minneapolis, a beautiful city in the summer, and luck was in my favor. My career was taking off, I had just bought a new car, and I was dating someone new—Grace, who I really liked. Grace showed me the world through new eyes. Her wit and wisdom challenged several false beliefs that I had been holding without realizing it. Being with Grace was like stepping into the ocean. The further I walked, the deeper I was immersed in warmth and compassion. She was beautiful, but her beauty was secondary to the vibe of her personality, which was even more compelling than her objectively attractive body.

Beautiful things can deceive and disappear, so I dated Grace with caution. I was intimidated by her sexiness and charm, and was afraid of doing something stupid, as I had done in the past, to blow the relationship. On our third date, we shared red wine and laughter at Chino Latino on Hennepin Avenue. We both lived nearby—her on Lyndale, me on Humboldt—in the Uptown neighborhood. After dinner I picked up the check and we walked into the moonlit street and kissed. A clumsy "sure" was all I could muster when she invited me to her apartment.

Expectations lead to disappointment. Driving to Grace's apartment, I had a lot of expectations, not only for the evening, but for our future together. I was getting ahead of myself. Soon, without realizing it, as I turned the corner on Lake Street, I was no longer enjoying the experience as it happened. I was anticipating results. I was looking ahead—to having sex, to having a girlfriend—which created an unnecessary pressure. My thoughts and actions became forced, and less natural than they had been earlier in the night. It was a small mistake. Sometimes that's all it takes.

I parked my car on Lyndale, and soon we were in her bedroom. She lit a candle, played a song by Frank Ocean on her MacBook, and dimmed the lights. We kissed slowly and undressed quickly, and lay down naked on her white sheets. And then . . . nothing. I kissed her again with forced passion. Nothing. I grabbed her body strongly, averted my eyes, and gazed at her naked skin. Contrary to the energetic connection I had felt for Grace earlier, now I was oversexualizing her in my mind, like a porn star or stripper, not someone whom I was falling in love with. Still nothing.

Oh no, I thought. *What is happening? I only drank two glasses of wine. This cannot be happening. Not with her.* My determination was hard, but my body was not. "Just give me a second," I said. Famous last words.

If there is a graceful way to react in this situation, I still don't know it. My manhood felt like it had been revoked. The truth is that I was too focused on results—having great sex with Grace—which took me out of my body and into my mind, and distracted me from the natural flow of the present moment. Sexual connection requires two people to be mindfully present to experience a shared energy. My mind was elsewhere, so my body followed. Within minutes, all of me was elsewhere—in my car driving home. More than just my tail was hiding between my legs.

Success (and failure) is a habit.

Every baseball player knows that home runs don't come from chasing pitches. Home runs happen when the batter and the swing are in flow together. For this to happen, the batter must maintain Zen-like focus all season and give undivided attention to each pitch as it comes. Every moment matters—the practice, the rituals, deep breathing, knowing the pitcher, choosing the right time to swing. "Stay loose," great hitters say. "Don't feel the pressure. Slow down and stay in the moment."

Results never happen in isolation; they are
a mirror reflection of our state of mind.
Failure is a habit. So is success.

Success—in baseball, sex, and life—happens when we cultivate a strong inner presence. Think about your goals. Do you want to earn a lot of money, raise great children, or maybe find the perfect partner? Goals are important because they keep us engaged and motivated. But our goals become obstacles when we fixate on the end result at the expense of the process. Results never happen in isolation; they are a mirror reflection of our state of mind. Failure is a habit. So is success. For example, sex does not begin when you take off your clothes. Sex is a form of interpersonal communication—including conversation, body language, and eye contact—that begins as soon as you enter the presence of another. If two people cannot establish an energetic connection with their clothes on, then no amount of lust or desire can elevate the connection when the clothes come off.

How we have sex is a reflection of how we live. When we live mindfully, we have sex mindfully. When we live absently, we have sex absently. When we are fully connected with ourselves, we can fully connect with others. When we maintain a focused inner presence and release attachments to results, we find joy in everything we do because our actions will be aligned with purpose.

The journey and destination are one.

"Nothing has happened in the past; it happened in the Now. Nothing will ever happen in the future; it will happen in the Now."

— ECKHART TOLLE

Life happens in the moment. There is nowhere but here and no time but now. Our society is strongly Ego-driven, and strives for results above all else. In doing so, we become distracted from the here and now. Schools, for example, place higher importance on test scores than on quality of learning. Businesses, driven by competition, value profit margins more than customer satisfaction. Athletes value personal glory more than the art of playing the game. Both men and women, including myself, often place greater importance on the pleasure of sex than on the energetic exchange of which sex is only a part.

What happens when society values results at the expense of process? Pressure happens. This pressure becomes an excuse for corruption. Work stops being fun. We move from a state of flow into a state of forced effort.

A corporation, for example, may choose to make a bad product or outsource production to third-world slave labor, because investors expect quarterly profits and quality is too expensive to maintain. A school, under pressure to show results, will push children into a competitive mind-set at an early age, forcing standardization instead of allowing each child to learn at the right pace for their personal growth. When process is forced, performance suffers. The journey and destination are aspects of the same motion, the swing of the bat and the hit of the ball.

"Only results matter," the Ego says. "I must seek validation for my work because I am unable to simply stand in my power." This perspective is backward. Results, both good and bad, are the reflection of our inner presence. When we chase results based on neediness, the outcome will be a reflection of our neediness. But when we focus with intention, moment by moment, and remain connected with the quiet space between our thoughts, the outcome will be a reflection of our intention.

Who knows, you might even get lucky.

Outside my hometown, Redwood Falls, Minnesota

CHAPTER 5

I NEED TO DEFEND MYSELF

Growing up in Redwood Falls, a small town in southwest Minnesota, there was a small dog, Snapper, living in my neighborhood. Snapper belonged to a family on the other side of the railroad tracks, on the east side of town near the soybean fields. But the whole neighborhood claimed Snapper as its own. Redwood Falls was a safe town. Kids were allowed to roam freely in the streets, into the woods, down the tracks, toward the river, and to the top of the waterfall—where we leaped into the water below. Snapper followed close behind and visited homes at his leisure. He was the affable neighborhood mascot, enjoying scraps of food where they were given and leading us bravely into imaginary battles, our honorary captain, time and time again.

Snapper's attitude changed around other dogs, especially bigger dogs, and most dogs were bigger than Snapper. Around other dogs, Snapper became nervous. His back arched upward and his shaggy eyebrows curved down. His tail, usually spinning like a helicopter propeller, stopped wagging and his tiny fangs appeared. It's not that Snapper did not like other dogs. He did. But he had a sneaky suspicion that other dogs did not like him. Snapper, small and scruffy as he was, had an inferiority complex with bigger canines, even nice ones. He barked in a valiant but fruitless effort to convince animals within earshot that he was not, in spite of his paltry stature, to be taken lightly.

We had to admire his spunk, but we felt bad seeing Snapper so defensive and guarded.

Making enemies out of shadows.

The Ego is a lot like Snapper (but less shaggy and cute). It lives in a world of perceived danger. Even when we are perfectly safe, the Ego invents false narratives of danger and victimization, causing our thoughts to be anxious and our actions defensive.

Living in New York City, where I eventually returned after leaving Culebra and have been living ever since, this happens to me all the time. Everyone, it seems, is better looking than me. Smarter too. Sometimes I think I'm the only person living in Manhattan who did not attend an Ivy League university. All men seem taller and have perfect heads of hair. When I am not paying attention to my thoughts and remembering to be mindful, these observations, even if exaggerated, make me insecure and defensive. And feeling defensive causes me to act rudely to both friends and strangers.

Life is an uphill battle, I think, *so I better protect myself.* No more holding doors. No more friendly gestures. Kindness is too risky. Everything, according to my Ego, is in danger—my finances, my career, my relationship, my peace of mind—so I feel compelled to launch a preemptive strike, barking at the world to prove my bite.

When I remember to hold a neutral state of mind—not seeking pleasure or avoiding pain—and stand in my own power, I do not have the same insecurities, even though my surroundings are the same. My thoughts, rather than becoming defensive, remain at peace with my neighbors, the city, myself, and the universe.

Acting defensively gives the Ego a momentary sense of security because the Ego feels safe when the mind is fearful and on guard. But the security of fear is soon broken. What the Ego does not understand is that reality is a reflection of our inner state. Thinking and behaving in a defensive manner is a cycle that sustains fear rather than eliminating it.

The universe returns whatever our thoughts project. Therefore the best defense against emotional and psychological danger is to live and act from a place of inner peace.

When we become defensive we allow ourselves to be guided by fear. But when we release the need to protect ourselves, we realize that the universe is a supportive place. Our courage protects us. The danger we face is not from one another, but rather from the irrational impulses of the mind. We are all bound together in the same mess. The people of New York City, no matter how handsome or educated, are just as insecure as I am, probably more. And the other dogs just wanted to be Snapper's friend.

The Ego mistakes
the world for a threat
and finds hope in fear
which soon shall cease

But wisdom gives up
the need for safety
and therein attains
a deeper peace

WHEN MY VIBES ARE WEAK

WHEN MY VIBES ARE STRONG

CHAPTER 6

I CAN'T CHANGE

C reativity is a weapon. Some people use charm to get ahead in life, others use money, or strong debate skills. But creativity has always been my weapon of choice, and it has opened doors to opportunities that would otherwise have been closed. But creativity is not all wine and roses, or a lazy way to pass the time. In fact, it can be an unwieldy and dangerous weapon. Creativity is romance with the unknown. It dances with secrets, makes love to uncertainty, and exposes our consciousness to the unknown inner self. Through this mysterious ceremony, something new is born. The unmanifest takes shape.

When an artist looks at an empty canvas, she does not see the vibrant hues and bold brushstrokes of the finished painting. That would be too easy. What she sees is doubt and failure looking her dead in the eye. Yet she continues.

The war of creativity is not fought on canvas. The war is fought inside the artist's mind. She can either allow uncertainty to defeat her, or she can overcome resistance and give birth to something new. This choice must be made again each day. Every time the artist (or writer or entrepreneur) looks at her canvas (or novel or business plan), she hears her Ego. "I am wasting my time," the Ego says. "I don't have what it takes." The only way to win and quiet the Ego is to silence the mind and make something. Creativity jumps over Ego.

Most of my life I have been an artist. This is not to say that I have always been a good artist, but I have always made things, or at least attempted to make things. After graduating high school, following an unhappy period at Southwest Minnesota State University, I walked away from college to pursue writing and painting full time, much to my parents' dismay. It was the only teenage rebellion I could muster, and only a few years too late. I dropped out of college because I hated the restrictions, and I was afraid of becoming another corporate robot. By the time I turned 23, I was living with my girlfriend in Syracuse, New York, where she was successfully enrolled in the theater program at Syracuse University, and I was (less successfully) working on my career as an artist.

Each morning I locked eyes with an empty canvas, or an empty notebook, and fought to overcome the resistance and fear that all creatives face. I had moved to Syracuse as a launching pad to eventually move to New York City, where I hoped my creativity would blossom into a career. But while I was big on dreams, I was short on direction. I could barely make ends meet in Syracuse, let alone the Big Apple. I was stuck—both emotionally and geographically—and was approaching the point where "depressed" would not be an absurd diagnosis. When my girlfriend left town to study abroad, it was the final nail in my coffin.

My frustration reached a crescendo one summer night when I decided to cut my losses and pack everything I owned into the backseat of my Cadillac Seville and drive 1,000 miles without stopping—listening to Modest Mouse and Bright Eyes on repeat—to my friend's apartment in Minneapolis, where I enrolled in design school while sleeping on his couch.

Design your own reality.

Fast-forward a few years. Design school was complete, and (after those few months working retail at Urban Outfitters) I was a professional graphic designer. Making the jump from starving artist to creative professional made me feel accomplished—for a while. I had changed how I thought about myself, which changed how I acted, which eventually transformed my professional life. But my interests continued to evolve. Like the snake who generates new skin under the aging layer, I was not finished growing.

In fact, nobody—regardless of age or profession—is finished growing. So we must continue learning. When we adopt what Zen Buddhism calls the "beginner's mind"—always open to new possibilities, never too smart to change our habits—we stay inspired and young. When we stop making a conscious effort to evolve, we get stuck.

Change is natural. Being stuck is unnatural.

My design career was accelerating, and after two years I was promoted to art director. But secretly I was beginning to feel stagnation. Obsessing over typography and Pantone colors—the process that once excited me—was beginning to drain me.

We all wear masks. Our identity is the mask we wear to show ourselves to the world. When I was young I wore the mask of an artist. When this mask no longer fit, I traded it for another mask—a designer. Our masks reveal part of us, but they do not represent our complete self. In a lifetime we wear many masks. When we outgrow one mask we replace it with a new one.

Gradually, I stopped identifying as a designer, and I knew it was time to make a change. But life was different now. I had a career. *Should I walk away and start over again?* I asked myself. *Or should I be safe and stay with the familiar?* I didn't know where I wanted to be, but I knew it was not where I was, so I started applying for new jobs, hoping my track record as a creative problem solver would be useful in other professions.

Every time I had a job interview I heard the same thing: "You have a nice design portfolio," they said. "But you are not qualified for this position." Meanwhile, back in the office, my discontent was rising. My frustration was causing me to push boundaries and treat others aggressively. The tension peaked on a cold February morning during a heated debate. "That is a terrible idea," I shouted at my boss. "I'm doing this project my way!" I was fired the next day.

Sure, I wanted to leave my job, but not like this. Suddenly I was facing unemployment, and my only career experience was in something I no longer wanted to do. Other design jobs were offered to me. It was tempting to take one, and more than once I almost said yes. But ultimately I decided that if I took another job that did not give me space to evolve into who I wanted to become, I would fall back into the same stuck pattern. It would be an uphill battle, but I knew that this was my opportunity to change.

"Don't be stupid," my Ego said. "People never change. Trying to evolve into somebody new is a waste of time. Do yourself a favor and take another design job. Transformation is a joke."

"Actually, people do change," my Higher Self said. "Transformation is not only real, it is your birthright. At some point you changed from your child self to become who you are now. The ability to expand has not left you. Your past does not dictate your future unless you allow it to. Change is natural. Being stuck is unnatural."

"Maybe so," my Ego said. "But I have invested too much time and energy into my current life to change now. I have responsibilities and obligations."

"Life is always changing," my Higher Self said. "And so are you. Your current life is similar to a small boat that carried you across the sea from one land to another. What happens to the boat when you reach land? Do you stay inside the boat, or do you step out and explore? When you arrive on land, there is no value in staying inside the boat. This does not mean the journey was a waste of time. It was exactly what you needed to arrive where you are now. Give thanks to the boat and continue moving. Everything you have learned prepares you for what happens next."

A new version of you.

Change can be terrifying because it brings the possibility of failure. "What will other people think?" the Ego says. "Will they judge me? It's probably safer to stay the same." Well, not really. The world is changing at a rapid pace. The rules of the old economy, top-down and linear, are breaking down and being rebuilt in the decentralized image of the Aquarian Age where everybody can be a leader. Having a "beginner's mind" is not fluffy Buddhist philosophy. It's a career advantage. Now more than ever before, you have permission to drop your old mask and become the version of yourself you want to be.

Whenever we change, there will be people around us, those who are stuck themselves, who may resent or pass judgment on our change. This is normal. Consider these voices validation that you are doing something that matters. The only opinion that matters is the voice inside yourself when you lie down to go to sleep. When your head hits the pillow, are you at peace with yourself? If yes, the opinions of others are merely background noise. If no, it might be time for a new routine, however uncomfortable that change may be.

The only thing that stops us from changing is our fear of embracing the unknown. Our reality is maintained by our mental, usually subconscious, commitment to the way things are. Before we can change, we must create space in our lives by releasing attachment to the past. This requires letting go of old thoughts and beliefs. When we release our attachment to what no longer serves us, old habits fade into the background like memories. When we shake our fear of uncertainty, change is not only possible; it is inevitable.

"But I can't change," the Ego says. "My thoughts and habits are all I know. It's too late for me to become somebody new."

"Your power to evolve does not expire," the Higher Self says. "There is no age limit for transformation. You are only responsible for the present—not the past. Life is the process of discovering your identity and stepping into yourself. Your current reality is only a guidepost, a milestone, on the path toward who you are becoming."

It takes work to progress.

"But change is hard," the Ego says. "There are too many obstacles."

This is true. Change is usually met with obstacles. These obstacles—such as other people or mental habits—are the residue from our old life attempting to hold us back. But when we examine our limitations, we usually discover simple ways to navigate past them. Having a dream is not enough. We need a strategy. Our inner vision is too important to leave to chance.

When I no longer self-identified as a designer, I took a strategic approach to reinventing my career. My first step was finding leaders in fields I was interested in pursuing—such as business, strategy, branding, and entrepreneurship—and setting up informational interviews to ask questions and understand the steps they took to become successful. These meetings taught me an important lesson: No problem is unique. No matter what I was facing, somebody else had overcome a similar challenge. Other people's challenges, I realized, could be shortcuts for my own solutions.

These conversations inspired me to rethink my job résumé. I no longer wanted to be a designer, but I realized that there was a wealth of knowledge within my design experience that could be applied to other fields. For example, I had worked with a range of clients and business models. Check. I had conducted research into different industries in order to understand how a brand should be positioned within its market. Check. I had given presentations and sold ideas to clients. Check. When I evaluated the thinking behind my job experience, I realized that I already had the answers; I simply needed to reframe the question.

Soon I had a job interview that clicked, and I was hired by a creative agency as a brand strategist. More than my career changed. My thinking changed. I learned how to apply creativity in new ways. Above all, I learned that my biggest limitation had been my self-perception.

Imagine the ideal version of yourself. What do you look like? How do you sound? What words do you use? What do you do for a living? Who do you spend your time with? Visualize the life you would choose if your current circumstances were not a factor. Now step toward it. Small steps are okay. Just step toward it. You may not see results right away. Just step toward it. Don't be afraid to stand in your power. Step toward it. Everybody is a work in progress, and it takes work to progress.

CHAPTER 7

I'M NOT CREATIVE

E very time I start a new creative project—this book for example, or an advertising campaign—I think the same thing: *This is going to be awesome.* This wave of excitement stays until I hit the first inevitable roadblock. After the second or third roadblock, my excitement usually inverts into doubt: *This is harder than I thought.* And as I evaluate my sketches of half-baked ideas, my dread progresses: *This is terrible,* which spirals into a criticism of my self-worth, *I am terrible.* And yet I continue—partly out of stubborn pride, partly because I am constantly searching for the next breakthrough, but mostly because continuing is my job. At some point the wave breaks. I stand back and observe my progress. *This is working,* I think, and continue building on that momentum until I am satisfied, or, more likely, until the project is due. I exhale and my thoughts come full circle: *That was awesome.*

Creativity is not magic. Imagination is not a privilege reserved for artists and geniuses. Anyone, at any given time, can be creative, because creativity is a process. The benefit of spending years working as a creative professional—where ideas are delivered on demand—is that after a while you figure out the process. You crack the code.

The secret, it turns out, is not waiting for inspiration to strike. The secret is rubbing two sticks together until fire has no choice but to show up. Chuck Close had the right idea. "Inspiration is for amateurs," he said. "The rest of us just show up and get to work." The work is the process of transforming imagination into reality. Imagination by itself is a fantasy. In order to become useful, imagination must leave the world of fantasy and enter the world of reality. This is done by channeling imagination through the workshop of manifestation—from dreaming to thinking to brainstorming to planning to executing—and sharpening the idea, from nebulous to concrete, toward gradually higher fidelity. Imagination is a necessary starting point, but making it real is the art.

Turning imagination into reality.

Stage one: Imagine

1. **Clear your mind of preconceived limitations.**
    In historic cultures, medicine men called shamans would heal others by moving energy through themselves into their patient's body. In order to create space within themselves for the healing energy to flow, they went through a self-cleansing process of emptying their bodies of toxins and negative energy. Being creative is being a shaman of ideas. Before we can solve a problem, we must quiet the Ego by shifting our mind-set from information to imagination. A cluttered mind blocks the motion of creativity. A clean mind—empty of preconceived limits— allows space for solutions to flow.

2. **Dream outside your comfort zone.**
    In the imagination stage, no idea is a bad idea. This is your chance to dream big—prior to the annoying logistics of execution—so go for it.

The first thing I do in a creative brainstorm is unleash a barrage of funny and ridiculous ideas. The point of this exercise is to shake myself and my team out of our comfort zone. The best ideas are risky. If an idea scares me, it's probably good.

3. **Don't rush solutions.**
   There is a Zen saying: "First thought, best thought." Sometime this is true. But usually the intuition of our first thought is a good direction, but not quite the final answer. Amateurs stop at their first idea. Professionals are comfortable wading in the muck of uncertainty until the challenge is fully solved. Solutions must be discovered, not forced. An incomplete solution will cause more problems down the road. It's okay to not know everything. Embrace uncertainty. Wander.

Stage two: Strategize

4. **Break your idea into small steps.**
   Ideas don't turn into reality instantaneously. The manifestation from ethereal to tangible happens in phases. Once you have an idea, the next step is mapping out the process of bringing your idea to life. The blueprint comes before the foundation, which comes before the construction, which comes before the decoration. Start small. Don't worry about perfection. Refine as you go.

5. **Foresee obstacles. Navigate accordingly.**
   Creativity rarely travels, as the crow flies, directly from the starting point to the finish

line. On the path to execution, you are sure to encounter roadblocks, monsters, trolls, and bad weather to test your moxie. Keep moving. This is merely a test. Obstacles can be avoided, or at least mitigated, when foreseen. Keep your head up. Watch for icebergs.

6. **Give yourself a deadline.**
Ideas require fuel to progress. Deadlines create an urgency that pushes ideas forward. You can imagine all day and never make progress. But the right amount of pressure—not too much pressure, which makes us react with fear— pushes creativity into overdrive and forces us to reach solutions we would otherwise be too lazy to see. Ideas should start with a dream and end with a bullet.

Stage three: Get shit done

7. **Don't wait for inspiration. Keep working.**
Ideas needs action to thrive. When you're ready to execute, the time for waiting is over. When you wait for inspiration to strike like some lucky bolt of lightning, you delay the action that fuels new ideas. Inspiration is attracted to hard work. Not feeling inspired? Start anyway. Allow the process to guide you, even if you don't know where you are going. Action is the best inspiration.

8. **Focus on effort. Drop expectation.**
The creation process is a holy battlefield. You are squared off, mano a mano, against your demons. A steady focus on the present moment will keep

you in the zone. Doubt and fear, like secret agents across enemy lines, will surely creep in. That's okay. Instead of fighting them, ignore them. Doubt and fear only win when you give them space to grow. Focus on the task at hand and drop attachment to results. You are only responsible for your effort.

9. **Enjoy the process (it's all process).** There is no beginning or end to creativity. The cycle lives in perpetual rotation. Amateurs feel pressure to finish, to get it right, to win, to impress. Professionals know better. Professionals understand that the goal is not as important as the process. The game is long. Failure along the way is expected. Everybody has different degrees of talent and experience, but the process of turning imagination into reality is available to everyone. There is an invisible vortex of ideas and imagination that floats beyond our senses. When we clear our minds and trust the unknown, anyone can access and channel this vortex. Creativity is the science of making the unseen real.

EVERY PERSON
I MEET
IS A
REFLECTION
OF MYSELF

CHAPTER 8

I'M WORRIED

There was once a wise farmer who lived in a small village tending his crops. One day his horse ran away unexpectedly into the mountains. The farmer waited all day for the horse to return, but it did not come back.

Upon hearing the news, the farmer's neighbors came to visit. "How terrible," they said.

"We'll see," the farmer said.

The next morning, to the farmer's surprise, the horse returned, accompanied by three other strong and healthy horses it had met in the mountains.

"How wonderful. You are very lucky," the neighbors exclaimed.

"We'll see," the farmer said.

The following day, the farmer's son decided to ride one of the new horses. The horse was wild, and the boy was thrown off the horse and fell hard onto the ground, breaking his leg.

"How sad," the neighbors said, offering sympathy once again for the farmer's misfortune.

"We'll see," the farmer said.

The next day, military officials arrived in the village to draft young men into the army. Seeing that the farmer's son's leg was broken, the military officials granted him permission to avoid the war. The neighbors congratulated the farmer on his good luck.

"We'll see," the farmer said.

Have you ever worried about something, and allowed your worry to consume you, only to later discover that your worry was unfounded? This happens to me all the time. Our human capacity to perceive is limited by our five senses, which causes us to miss the big picture. In other words, what we do not know is much greater than what we know. The Ego fears the unknown and jumps to conclusions in order to feel a false sense of certainty. Worry is based on assumptions, and the Ego, from a place of fear and attachment, tries to convince us that its assumptions are true. This is the origin of worry. Worry is the Ego's way of satisfying itself with an answer, any answer, no matter how irrational and unlikely it may be.

Like most people, I worry a lot. I realize that I shouldn't— that worry only helps to manifest the outcome that I am worried about—and yet I worry anyway, usually subconsciously. I worry about my career, my relationships, having enough money, missing the subway from Brooklyn to Manhattan, and more. Anything that I can imagine going wrong, I worry about. But worry is dangerous. When we worry—which is seeing life through a lens of fear—we misread reality and make mental mistakes.

For example, I might worry that you are angry with me, although in reality you are not. My worry causes me to become defensive. You will then observe my defensive behavior and make assumptions about my actions. Because you do not understand the reasons for my behavior—that I am merely trying to protect myself—you will assume that I am angry with you. Now we are both engaged in mutual anger based on false assumptions caused by worry. The truth is that I will never know what is happening inside your mind, and you will never know what is happening inside my mind. There is very little that we know for certain, and the Ego's bravado in believing otherwise causes a domino effect of miscalculations.

Reality is a flower and thoughts are the seeds. The thoughts we plant influence the reality that grows.

It is common in our society to believe that more thinking is always better. This is not always so. Intelligence is an incredible tool, but intelligence does not equal wisdom, and overthinking can be just as harmful as underthinking. Overthinking is a sickness that creates paranoia and worry. When we overthink, we make up scenarios in our mind and convince ourselves that these scenarios are true. Without enough data to make a proper assessment, the Ego hijacks our imagination and jumps to fear-based conclusions. Fear + imagination = worry. Worry is the dark side of the imagination.

We often feel pressure to have all the answers, but admitting what we don't know is a sign of wisdom. Try saying it: "I don't know"—or as the farmer said, "We'll see." The universe works in mysterious ways. Embracing this mystery gives us calm within the storm of uncertainty. Instead of overthinking and jumping to false conclusions, as I have done in the past, I have slowly learned to make peace with uncertainty. I don't need all the answers all the time. Most of reality is unknowable to human perception, and that is okay. When we wait in stillness, and drop the need for certainty, a deeper understanding of the situation and the best path ahead become intuitively known.

Worry is wishing for what we don't want.

Thoughts are magnets. We attract into our lives the people and events that align with our mental and emotional vibrations. When I am worried, I am more likely to experience circumstances that validate my worry. This has nothing to do with magic and everything to do with habit. Our subconscious beliefs inform our thoughts, and what we think on a regular basis reinforces those beliefs. This pattern of thought and belief programs our internal reality. We then see the world from the biased premise of our thoughts and beliefs, which tunes our perception toward external events that match our inner state of being. Over time we become what we believe. This so-called law of attraction is merely the mind's ability to filter reality through the bias of belief. We all do this every day.

Reality is a flower and thoughts are the seed. The thoughts we plant influence the reality that grows. Would you rather grow a garden of sunflowers or thorns? Your mind has the capacity to produce both. Once the flower of our reality has grown, we are unable to change its nature with force. All change happens within the soil. We can only transform our reality (the plant) at the level of our thoughts (the seeds). Because we cannot control the outer world, there is nothing to worry about. Instead, we can return to the soil and start planting different seeds.

You'll see.

Sitting on Culebra, watching the tide rise and fall, I was worried about my future. "This is terrible," my Ego said. "I don't have a home, or any money, and I don't know what will happen next. Nothing good can come from this."

I took a deep breath and continued looking at the water. *Inhale. Exhale. Inhale. Exhale.* A cool breeze touched my face.

"What are you worried about?" my Higher Self said. "You don't have the data to understand how this story will end, so don't jump to conclusions. Let go of your Ego's need for answers. Maybe there is a plan in place that you cannot see. Remain neutral to the waves in your mind, even when they come crashing down. You'll see."

CHAPTER 9

LIFE IS HEAVY

You could say I had a type. Most girls I've dated have shared a few common traits. Historically I have been attracted to girls with a vaguely bohemian style, literary types with a sort of unspoken and unknowable mystery, dark-haired deep thinkers, old souls with a tinge of sadness behind their eyes. Emotional sensitivity is a sign of character. There is nothing like looking into a woman's eyes and seeing decades, maybe even centuries, of wonder and mystery hidden beneath a stoic, even classical, composure. There is a certain beauty to being worn down by the road. But Ashley was different. Ashley was light.

We were an experiment in opposites. In conversation, I tend to riff on weighty, often esoteric, philosophical topics that have been known to kill the mood during small talk and dinner parties. *Who is really running America? If individuals have free will, why do the masses always choose conformity? What is the purpose of life?* But whenever I went too deep, Ashley merely laughed and changed the subject. She was absolutely free and had no interest in being weighed down by debate or analysis. Her goal was simple: live each moment with as much joy as possible.

Without trying, Ashley pushed me outside my comfort zone into a place sunnier than I was accustomed to being. My thoughts could not be burdensome with Ashley because she did not speak my language of doubt and regret. She shed light on every dark corner my mind would wander.

The unbearable heaviness of being.

I was born in a small Minnesota town molded by practical values and a solemn sense of responsibility. Conditioned from an early age to view life as inherently burdensome, our no-nonsense attitude was devoid of irony. The demeanor of the "Land of 10,000 Lakes" could result from the cold winters, or maybe a lingering sense of guilt from the 1860s Sioux massacres, or perhaps the bad luck of the Minnesota Vikings. However it came to happen, we are committed to our burden. Too much fun is not to be trusted. In Minnesota, we wear our worry on our sleeve.

Ashley helped me rethink everything. For her, fun was life's highest virtue. Whenever I perceived a problem, or something that needed to be fixed, it did not register with Ashley—as though we were different animals who heard different frequencies—and things that worried me blew past her like breeze over a tulip. This did not make sense to my Ego. The Ego takes comfort in heaviness because when life is heavy, the Ego has an important job—the job of being worried, which feeds its self-importance. "Life is hard," the Ego says. "So I must remain alert. What if I run out of money? What if I lose my job? What if people think I'm stupid? The weight of my burden holds my life in balance. If I put my guard down everything will fall apart. I need my problems because they validate my existence."

Ashley's life was easy. I wanted to live that way too, and considered the difference between lightness and heaviness. Whenever my Ego perceived life as a struggle, I heard Ashley's voice in my head offer a polite rebuttal. "Don't be so dramatic," I imagined her to say—not with condemnation or judgment, but with the professionalism of a doctor identifying the root cause of pain. "Life is not so serious. Whatever problems you are experiencing only exist within the context of your perception. No problem is a big deal. What exactly is at stake? Life is a gift that comes and goes, and your worries have no significance outside your own mind. So let them go. Your Ego is inventing problems to justify your heaviness. But heaviness itself is the problem. Life is a story we tell ourselves, so make the story good."

Stop making sense.

"The only way to deal with an unfree world is to become so absolutely free that your very existence is an act of rebellion."

— ALBERT CAMUS

"Living freely is not logical," the Ego says. "When I analyze life with a critical eye, there are many reasons to take life seriously. It would be irresponsible to be light and happy when so many people are unhappy and the infrastructure of society is crumbling. My heavy state of existence acknowledges the real problems facing the world. Bad things happen. This is reality. It doesn't make sense to be happy in the face of such burdens."

"Your circumstances are not always a choice," the Higher Self says. "But living with burden is always a choice. Struggle is a matter of perception. When you see life from a heavy point of view, your perception tunes into a heavy version of reality. When you change your point of view, reality also changes. Everyone struggles, but you have the choice to take your struggle lightly. This may not be logical, but that is okay. There is an energetic intelligence in the universe—invisibly guiding and connecting all things—that supersedes the intelligence of mental logic. Look at the idea of dancing. Logically, dancing does not make sense. You twist and turn to the rhythm of the music, and allow the energy of your body to transcend the logic of your mind. And what is accomplished? Nothing. Dancing has no reason. And yet, when you suspend your logic and trust the body, something clicks. The reason, it turns out, is the lack of reason."

If it gets too heavy, put it down.

When the student is ready, the teacher will come. Our teachers usually appear in the least expected ways as the least expected people. Ashley was a teacher. She taught me to accept happiness without the burden of worry and judgment, and I am grateful for this lesson. Our breakup was amicable. Our opposing worldviews had held our relationship in balance—for a while—but the balancing act eventually became too tedious to manage.

The act of receiving love, both from others and ourselves, can feel like a bright light. Sometimes this light is too bright to handle. When light shines on our scars, our sensitivity is revealed and we feel exposed. This exposure is painful. But learning to accept the brightness of love is how we heal our inner darkness. All too briefly, Ashley showed me what it means to shine awareness into the darkness of life until there is nothing left to hide. I'm still learning how to practice this lesson.

On our last night together I rolled over in bed and asked her the question I had been thinking for months. "Your life is effortless," I said. "How do you float the way you do?"

Ashley laughed. "Because I take myself lightly," she said.

CHAPTER 10

I HATE MY JOB

I arrived to work early and poured black coffee. It was Wednesday. Sunlight poured into my office window as I sat down at my computer, took a sip of coffee, and checked my e-mail. Between the banal, "donuts in the kitchen," and the urgent, "the client wants to fire us," I came across a company announcement. I had known for weeks that my company, a creative agency based in New York City, was planning to open a new office downtown. What I did not know until I checked my e-mail was that my department was moving to the new location. I was disappointed, but took the news in stride. *This happens all the time in business,* I thought. *It's no big deal.* Truthfully I felt helpless, but I accepted my fate without complaint, and told myself that I would find happiness wherever I was thrown. After all, the only thing changing was my location. My job would be the same. So I thought.

"Did you hear the news?" Emma asked. Emma also worked in the creative department.

"We are moving downtown," I replied. "I saw the e-mail."

"There's more," Emma said. "We are being absorbed into the analytics department. And we'll have a new boss. By this time next month, our jobs will look very different."

My emotions were a cocktail of confusion and devastation. I had returned to New York City from Culebra six months earlier and was trying hard to assimilate the lessons I had learned about my Ego into my professional life. I was just starting to feel comfortable at my new agency, and my team was providing clients with good creative work. Now everything was changing, and my job was in limbo. Two weeks later it was official. I moved offices with a box of personal items in my hands and an annoyed look on my face.

"How can the creative team be managed by the analytics team?" I complained to Emma. "It doesn't make sense. Data should support creative ideas, not the other way around. Imagination cannot be reduced to an algorithm."

Things looked bad and soon became worse. I realized that I would be reporting to a new boss, Mark, who was well known around the office, not for the confidence he inspired, but for being—to use a word often quoted in relation to his name—an asshole. Mark was not a leader. He was a manager. And his management style resembled an overlord under pressure to maximize the productivity of a sweatshop. Instead of encouraging us to develop our talents and become the best version of ourselves, he did everything in his power to fill us with fear and have us obey him without question. Machiavelli would have been proud.

Creativity blossoms when the mind is free. Working with fear is a cage on our thoughts. My new working environment was governed by fear and resource scarcity. There was no trust, and employees blamed each other in order to stay out of trouble. For the first time in my life, my mind felt imprisoned. My energy drained like a leaky faucet and my ideas were at the mercy of data reports. When the left brain is king, the right brain becomes the jester. I felt like a joke.

Why do you show up for work?

What is the motivation that causes us to get out of bed every day? Is it the demanding voice of fear? Or is it the pursuit of purpose and self-actualization? When we work because of fear, we will fail to make meaningful progress in our career. Even worse, we will leave work and go home in a state of misery. But when purpose is the driving factor of our work, the outcome will be inspired. This is not always easy, but it is always necessary. More than our career is at stake. Our dreams are at stake. Under pressure to produce results, we often forget the dreams that inspired us to begin our careers in the first place, and over time we begin showing up tired and uninspired. Clock in, check out, repeat. "I hate my job," the Ego says. "But I have bills to pay and things to buy. Besides, dreams are for children. It would be nice to have a career that fulfilled my purpose, but that's not realistic."

"Work is not about money and security," the Higher Self says. "Work is about engaging with others in order to actualize your purpose. Money and security mean nothing when you are unhappy and stressed. You become unhappy and stressed when you follow the expectations of the status quo at the expense of your own vision. Your job does not matter. You are not defined by your job title. What you do is not as important as how you do it. Your career becomes meaningful to the degree that you actualize your inner truth and reveal that truth to those around you. Your job is a classroom to learn and teach. What you learn and teach are more than job skills; they are the value of shared humanity. This value exchange is unseen, but is the true purpose of work."

A quest with no vision.

There was a time when children around the world became adults by going through a social rite of passage called a spiritual journey. This tradition symbolized official entrance into the community. In some Native American cultures, for example, children who reached a certain age (usually around

15) embarked on an adventure into solitude—called a vision quest—to discover their purpose in the world. On his vision quest, the initiate would journey into the wilderness for several days and listen for guidance from the Higher Self, often spoken through the language of nature. He studied the birds, the river, the forest, the relationship between predator and prey, and in doing so attained a greater understanding of the complexity and synchronicity of the world into which he was born. Upon return, the child was empowered with a new sense of vision and responsibility, and he was ready to fulfill his role within the community.

In modern society, the idea of the vision quest is considered nonsense, and children are left to enter the gates of society on a quest with no vision. The wilderness we enter is not the forest. It is the economy. Our guide is not the Higher Self. It is universities and internships. Instead of spending time alone in contemplation, we look into computer monitors with the same intensity and longing for purpose as Native American seekers looking into the wilderness, hoping to find an answer within the light of the screen. We don't always like it, but it pays the bills, so we keep showing up.

The stress of the workday often leaves us feeling stuck inside a system that we did not choose and reduced to a number within the noise. In the race to advance our careers, we barely have time to enjoy our friends and family, let alone pursue the purpose of our Higher Self. I understand this dilemma because as a creative kid who found himself spinning in the tornado of corporate America, I have lived it. I have walked into many offices questioning why, and counted the hours I was giving away in support of somebody else's dream. Unable to find solace, I blamed my job for my unhappiness. My dejection led to frustration, which led to depression. I sleepwalked for eight hours a day, waiting to return home to pour whiskey over ice and stare aimlessly at the internet in an attempt to cloud my memory of the day.

At the time I did not realize a simple truth: We give ourselves the same emotions we invest in others. We receive love from ourselves when we give love to others. We receive apathy from ourselves when we give apathy to others. We always get a fair return on our investment.

Trust wherever you are.

There is a parable in Stoic philosophy about a dog and a wagon. Life is a moving wagon, the parable says, and every person is a dog tied to the wagon with a rope. When the wagon moves, it pulls us forward, whether we like it or not. We have two choices. We can run alongside the wagon or we can resist and be dragged. The first choice requires a little work. But the second choice is more painful. And either way we are going to the same place. The wagon always leads us where we need to be. Life is not always fair, but it never makes mistakes. When we become frustrated and curse our fate, this is hard to believe. But wherever we are—the mountain, the valley, the feast, the war—we are moving toward self-actualization according to the laws of our unique dharma. Every soul has a different lesson to learn, and our present conditions do not determine our destiny. One day we are slaves and the next day we are kings. The wheel is always spinning and we are always in a position to create inner peace and stillness.

"That can't be true," the Ego says. "What about circumstances that make self-actualization impossible—like poor health and poverty?"

"Every struggle has a purpose," the Higher Self says. "Sometimes that purpose is exploration. Consider the ancient pioneers. They faced great tribulations and darkness—including the possibility of sickness, death, cannibalism, storms, sea monsters, and enemy tribes—in order to expand the horizons of humanity. Their journey was a struggle, yet they continued. They build settlements where once was only mystery and laid the foundation for a new world. You too are an explorer. Your purpose is uncharted territory. There are no maps and the road is unpaved. Will you face obstacles? Of course. But obstacles are merely the brush, thorns, and branches that must be removed as you blaze the trail toward a new horizon. And when you arrive, by turning your resistance into persistence, you will look back and understand that your struggle, because you had to rise above it, was the catalyst that awoke you from your conditioning to remember that your nature is to shine."

Everyone is on a different path. Your path is different from mine, and we each have unique lessons to learn and baggage to release. Our struggle teaches us how to let go. We all, even the purest among us, carry pockets of resistance in the corners of our minds, which is the residue of past energy that is no longer serving us. Even when our conscious mind moves beyond past experiences, the residue of old habits and beliefs remains, hidden within our subconscious like blind spots of the mind. We must investigate darkness in order to understand where light is needed. Our struggles allow us to examine these dark corners of consciousness and release pockets of stuck energy. If we avoid the hard work of life, we will never release the baggage that is holding us down. By loving our work, we learn to let go.

It is our nature to shine.

Trying to change the world is like walking into a wall
Changing ourselves transforms the wall into a door
Fighting to overcome "that which is" drives us insane
Releasing the need to fight raises us above the war

When my creative department moved downtown to work with Mark and the analytics team, acceptance and purpose were the last things on my mind. Frankly, I was pissed off, and blamed others for my unhappiness. But things eventually changed—not by changing my job, but by changing my thoughts. *What beliefs am I holding that make me feel stuck?* I wondered. Beliefs have energy. So do thoughts. Even physical matter can be broken down, and broken down again, until all that remains is energetic frequency. Because everything is energy, including ourselves, we cannot stay long in an environment—such as a job—that is not, on some level, our energetic match. We can only go (outside) where we already are (inside). Placing blame is counterproductive. The only way to transform our environment is to transform the frequency of our thoughts and beliefs. Our struggles, when we embrace them, help us examine and transcend the thoughts that hold us down. Therefore our greatest challenges are our greatest teachers, and there is value in every difficult moment.

Our life purpose starts wherever we are.
We cannot wait for circumstances to be perfect
because circumstances are never perfect.
The first step toward every dream was
taken by somebody who was stuck in
an environment they did not choose.

Consider the behavior of a light beam. When a light beam shines onto a surface, it shines without judgment or hesitation. If an object is placed onto the floor and blocks the light's path, the light does not resist or resent the object. It continues to shine without judgment or hesitation on whatever it encounters with equal dedication. The light beam's nature is to shine. It does not concern itself with what it shines upon.

It is also our nature to shine upon the world. When we have a goal, we must shine our light (which is our love and attention) upon that goal. And when an obstacle blocks our goal, we must continue to shine our light upon the obstacle. When we are disappointed, we must shine our light upon our disappointment. We must continue to shine in the face of obstacles because the light we shine is the light that guides our path.

Nature is a doctor who prescribes our reality
All things are assigned with purpose and care
If nature did not need it, we would not see it
So shine as the sun, equally on all that's there

All work is holy.

"Work is love made visible."

— KAHLIL GIBRAN

Our life purpose starts wherever we are. We cannot wait for circumstances to be perfect because circumstances are never perfect. The first step toward every dream was taken by somebody who was stuck in an environment they did not choose. We must begin living our purpose before our environment reflects this purpose. This is our cosmic test. "Can you live your purpose even when circumstances are not ideal?" the universe asks. "Can you act out your role before the stage is ready? If you pass the test, I will accommodate you with the right circumstances to match your attitude. But first, you must prove that you are committed to living your purpose internally before your external conditions are matched." If we want a profession that aligns with our purpose, we must begin with the job we have now.

All work is service. Think of yourself as a healer. Your co-workers, customers, and clients are the people you are assigned to serve and heal. Your role is important. It does not matter what you do. The cab driver has a mission every bit as valuable as the CEO. Your role is important because, no matter what you do, people are depending on you. You may not enjoy your work, but the work itself is not as important as the people you are assigned to serve. And yet, your current job is not your fate. Your role will eventually change as your consciousness changes. But at this moment you are being called to make an impact where you have been assigned. Instead of waiting for your job to be perfect, make your reaction to your job perfect. Show up every day as an act of service. Take what you are given and turn it into art.

The key to
success
is to pick
the lock.

CHAPTER 11

I ONLY BELIEVE
WHAT I CAN SEE

The classical Greek philosopher Plato, who studied in Athens under the tutelage of Socrates, is widely considered the brightest light in the history of Western thought. Plato's influence extends beyond the modern definition of philosophy. His thinking has been foundational in several disciplines, including politics, science, ethics, relationships, and spirituality. In Plato's famous collection of work *The Republic*, written around 380 B.C.E., he shares one of his most enduring stories—the allegory of the cave. In the allegory of the cave, Plato compares the human experience to a group of people who have spent their entire lives inside a cave, their heads chained so they may only look forward at the same wall, day after day and night after night. Every day these people see shadows moving on the wall, and because they are unable to turn around and see the people and objects creating the shadows, they mistake the shadows to be the true, and only, reality. Their conception of reality is limited because their perspective is limited.

Humankind, according to Plato, is the same way. We are living in the darkness of half-truths, believing to see the whole truth, because we do not have the tools of perception to understand the full spectrum of reality. We only see the cave wall and are unable to perceive, or even conceptualize, the sun. Any claim about a reality beyond the confines of the cave is met with skepticism. "I only believe what I can see," the Ego says. "Nothing exists that is beyond my mind's capacity to understand."

Objective vs. subjective reality.

"If the doors of perception were cleansed, everything would appear to man as it is, infinite."

— WILLIAM BLAKE

Reality is a loaded word. Is there such a thing as objective reality, or is everything a matter of personal interpretation based on experience? Maybe both are true. Maybe an ultimate reality and a subjective reality both exist. Ultimate reality is the truest nature of the universe, all things, both material and energetic, in their ideal form and independent of our perception. Subjective reality, on the other hand, is the world as we experience it, the result of our localized perception of ultimate reality filtered through our tools of human perception.

At this stage of human evolution, ultimate reality is unknowable to us because we simply do not possess a wide enough range of consciousness to perceive its awesome scope. Perhaps science will one day get there, but today we are still in the infantile stages of mapping out the physical, not to mention metaphysical, spectrum of the universe. The best we can offer is metaphors and poetics, usually in the form of religious and revelatory half-truths, which hint at what we intuitively feel to be true—the greatness beyond us and part of us—but that we can neither articulate nor fully understand.

Because the terms of subjective reality are defined by our perception—we are, and life is, what we perceive—when we broaden our perception we will inevitably broaden our experience of reality. One of the primary data inputs for our subjective reality is information from our five senses—seeing, hearing, tasting, smelling, and touching. Our five senses are so convincing that we believe they represent ultimate reality. But on closer inspection, they don't. Ultimate reality exists far beyond our capacity to perceive it with our senses. Like shadows on the wall of a cave, human perception does not tell the whole story. Our senses are like a radio dial. They tune our perception to a specific frequency. We know the frequency of five senses as the material world. But in focusing our perception, our senses conceal more truth than they reveal.

the electromagnetic spectrum

gamma   X-ray   ultra violet   infrared   TV & radio   electric

visible light

Visible light (that which is perceivable by the human eye) consists of wavelengths between approximately 780 nanometers (7.80 x 10⁻⁹ m) and 390 nanometers (3.90 x 10⁻⁹ m) in size. In the context of the electromagnetic spectrum, this is next to nothing. In comparison, if we were to take the entire light spectrum and condense it to the size of the Mississippi River, which flows 2,340 miles from the top of Minnesota into the Gulf of Mexico, the portion that would be visible to the human eye is merely eight inches. We are unable to see most—in fact, nearly all—of the light that we know to exist because it is a frequency beyond our perception. The same is true for sound, smell, taste, and touch. We only experience a small percentage of what has been proven to exist. The rest is territory beyond our reach, the next frontier, a colossal world waiting to be discovered.

We are watching the motion of shadows inside the confines of a cave while all around us, invisible to the human eye, other dimensions—the cause of the shadows—are shuffling.

Cast a wider net.

"What's the big deal?" the Ego says. "We can't see gamma rays or infrared light, or hear sounds beyond our frequency, so why does it matter?"

Think of consciousness as a fishing net. When we cast a small net into the ocean, we will capture a small number of fish. The same is true when we cast a small net of consciousness into the ocean of reality. We will capture a small amount of information. But when we widen our net by expanding our thoughts and discarding limiting beliefs, we catch more information, and more ideas, and more inspiration. The answers are waiting when we have eyes to see them.

To expand our reality, we must have the courage to become pioneers of our perception. We must release what is small and known and trust what is big and unknown.

We are surrounded by a vortex of data and intelligence taking place on a wide spectrum of energetic frequencies—both above us and below us. Our subjective reality, filtered by the Ego, is able to perceive only a very small portion of this spectrum. Carl Jung described this vortex of unseen intelligence as the collective unconscious, an intuitive spring of knowledge, built up over the history of civilization, shared by all living women and men. The wider the net of our perception, the more we can tap into the collective unconscious and access knowledge (in the form of intuition and creativity) that would otherwise be out of reach. The Ego is afraid to cast a wider net because it fears venturing away from its comfort zone. It would be safer, the Ego believes, to live in a world of known limitations than to explore the boundaries of unknown possibilities. To expand our reality, we must have the courage to become pioneers of our perception. We must release what is small and known and trust what is big and unknown.

"Problems cannot be solved with the same mind-set that created them," Albert Einstein reportedly said. Our problems, both individual and global, also cannot be solved without first expanding the reach of our consciousness. Like shadows are the outcome of physical objects, the material world is the outcome of immaterial energy. Therefore our power as people does not come from things we can see (such as money and possessions). Our power comes from things we cannot see (such as presence and awareness). Our reality will always grow to fit the openness of our mind.

Discovery starts as imagination.

"I only believe what I can see," the Ego says. This belief is based on a limited understanding of reality. When we understand that the world is a reflection of our perception, a deeper truth is revealed: *we must believe before we can see.*

All science began as an idea. Facts grow from imagination. Success is born from beliefs. The terms *physical* and *nonphysical* are misleading. The difference between "physical" and "nonphysical" is not absolute; it is a matter of degree. They are different frequencies of the same buzzing non-stuff, a vibration that permeates all things with infinite detail and expansion. Nothing, it turns out, is not part of the same whole, although it wears an infinite number of masks. The surface ripples, but the ocean remains.

In the allegory of the cave, Plato compares the philosopher—the enlightened one—to someone who finally stands up, removes his chains, and departs from the cave. No longer a slave to limited perception, he sees for the first time the depth of reality beyond the shadows on the wall. When the philosopher sees the physical objects responsible for the shadows, and observes the light of the sun for the first time, his consciousness is fundamentally changed. He will never return to the false conceptions he once held to be true. Our lives, Plato said, are the same. We can choose to live inside a cave, and limit our perception to the shadows of external reality, or we can look within ourselves and move beyond the cave into the light of the unknown sun.

I used to doubt myself
and believe that everybody
else knew better than me
and I was better off
following them.

But here's the thing.
Nobody knows anything
and everybody everywhere
(even your boss and
your president)
is only pretending
to know.

So I don't doubt anymore.
I just allow the movie to play
and no longer ask
for permission.

CHAPTER 12

I'M A SPIRITUAL PERSON

"There was never any more inception than there is now,
Nor any more youth or age than there is now,
And will never be any more perfection than there is now,
Nor any more heaven or hell than there is now."

— WALT WHITMAN

It was Friday evening in New York City and swarms of people moved from sad office hours to bar happy hours, but I had other plans. Walking across the Garment District, I approached a spiritual center on 7th Avenue and walked inside, ready for my first meditation class. The lobby was elaborate, decorated with ornate tapestries, Buddha statues, and wooden pillars etched with symbols from myriad world religions. A flock of yogis, bearded and beaded, gave each other salutations using words and hand gestures I did not understand. My flannel shirt and Converse All Stars were conspicuous among the white linen tunics and prayer beads of the crowd. Some even wore turbans. *Where does one even buy a turban?* I thought, making a mental note to check Amazon later. The whole scene, decidedly insular as it was, made me feel out of place, but the rhythmic echo from the brass gong in the corner was relaxing, so I accepted my pillow and proceeded to the meditation room.

The room was large and we sat on the floor. The meditation class began. The first exercise involved the conscious control of breath. *Inhale. Exhale. Inhale. Exhale.* I could not tell if I was doing it right. *Inhale. Exhale. Inhale. Exhale.* After a few minutes, my mind relaxed and I no longer cared if I was doing it right. *Inhale. Exhale. Inhale. Exhale.* The details from my week, the stress of my job, and the noise of New York City began to evaporate into the void of thoughtless breathing. The atmosphere opened like a window and a calm breeze entered the room.

Wow, I thought. *Maybe there is something to this meditation stuff.* Then I remembered that I was not supposed to think anything. So I tried to stop thinking. Then I realized that I was thinking about not thinking, so I stopped thinking about that too. I focused on my breath. *Inhale. Exhale. Inhale. Exhale.*

Forty-five minutes later the meditation ended. I released one final exhale and opened my eyes. Everyone in class was more experienced in meditation than me. I still felt awkward, but I no longer cared. The room shared a moment of peaceful silence. The meditation teacher, an older man wearing a turban and no shoes, broke the silence by speaking into a microphone.

"Why do we practice meditation?" he asked. "Because meditation takes us inside. By going inside, and disconnecting from the world, we elevate our consciousness. Meditation teaches us to transcend the physical experience." He continued to speak about the separation between the material and the spiritual. "The world around us—including the temptations of sex, drugs, and possessions—is a distraction from spirit, which is truth. To live in the material world is to suffer. But rising above the material world sets us free."

I can't remember if my eyes rolled or if I only imagined they did. The teacher's words made an impact on me, but not the impact he had intended. He told us to elevate above the physical world. To me, this sounded—especially given his nervous tone—like escapism. I had enjoyed the meditation, and felt it had connected me on a deeper level to myself and those around me, including the material things that defined my physical reality. And now the teacher was saying that although everything is connected to the same expansive oneness, the physical world was something we needed to escape. This confused me. *Escape to where?* I wondered. *If everything is connected, as great spiritual teachers say, doesn't everything exist here and now, at all times, and in all dimensions? If everything is sacred, how can we pass judgment on the physical world?* During the next few days my thoughts returned often to the meditation class. *What does it mean to be a spiritual person?* I thought. I did not have an answer. But I did know—or at least I intuited—that separating the spiritual from the material seemed like an arbitrary distinction. Trying to escape reality, instead of accepting all things as aspects of an interconnected oneness, is another form of Ego. The Ego, it turns out, can wear a spiritual disguise.

Enlightenment is seeing light in all things.

"The problem is that Ego can convert anything to its own use, even spirituality."

— CHÖGYAM TRUNGPA

"I am special because I have a spiritual practice," the Ego says. "The world is full of bad ideas and bad people, but I am above them."

"Everything in life—the trees, the pavement, the storms, the success, the failure—has a purpose interrelated with all other things," the Higher Self says. "There is no reason to run away from your reality. When you remove the polarity of labels such as 'good' and 'bad,' you leave behind a state of judgment and move into a state of acceptance; here you can see that every challenge pushes you forward. There is nothing—no ideology or belief—more important than where you are here and now. There is no afterlife; there is *only life*. Life is one continuous flow of energy with no beginning or end, and no moment along the continuum is more sacred than another in this dimension or the next. Why worry about being spiritual? There is nothing else you can be."

"But life is full of sadness," the Ego says. "Even Buddha taught that life is suffering. I want to escape suffering and elevate to a higher consciousness. I want to be enlightened."

"Enlightenment is seeing light in all things," the Higher Self says. "The human experience is not complete without the spiritual experience. But the spiritual experience is also not complete without the human experience. Your humanity is an aspect of your consciousness. When you embrace your humanity, instead of trying to escape it, you will discover the messy perfection of daily life. Even shadows, after all, are created by light."

"But bad things happen," the Ego says. "How can I see the light when my life is unfair?"

"Imagine you are watching a movie," the Higher Self Says. "The hero of the movie is in trouble. The plot is tense and you feel afraid. Yet you do not turn off the movie. Why not? Because you understand it is only a movie. No matter what happens, even the worst possible outcome, you will leave the theater and everything will be okay. Before long the tension of the movie will be a distant memory. Life is like this movie. Conflict is essential to the plot. After all, a movie without conflict is not interesting. But there is no reason to be afraid or run away. Your material life is temporary, and all aspects—including drama, luxury, sex, and danger—are part of the same dream. You have nothing to transcend. You have everything to learn."

CHAPTER 13

THE CITY IS KILLING ME

Before Europeans arrived in North America, a group of indigenous people called the Lenapes was living in modern-day Delaware, New York, New Jersey, and Pennsylvania. The Lenapes (which translates to "the real people") lived off the land and tended it with the care of a momma bear caring for her cubs. And what land it was. Rich forest, dense with wildlife, was cut by rivers and streams and extended from the eastern seaboard beyond the western horizon. The prize jewel of this lush landscape was a small island, 13 miles long, tucked between two rivers that merged into the Atlantic Ocean. The island was called Mannahatta.

Mannahatta, which is modern New York City, was a place of ecological astonishment. Home to animal and plant diversity surpassing most national parks, it was a wildlife sanctuary which remained, apart from the occasional native wigwam and campfire, untouched by civilization. Foreshadowing the island's destiny as a global melting pot, bears, wolves, beavers, mountain lions, otters, elk, and over 230 types of birds co-inhabited 33 square miles of open air from present-day Inwood to Battery Park. Mannahatta was preserved by the Lenapes for centuries until a September afternoon in 1609 when a Dutch flyboat captained by Henry Hudson made a fortuitous right turn in the North Atlantic Ocean.

Henry Hudson's mission was believed to be a failure. He never discovered the Northwest Passage between the Netherlands and India that he had been commissioned to find. Yet failure can open doors that were not known to exist. Sailing into the nameless river, Henry Hudson's eyes widened as he considered the economic potential of the plentiful island. His crew disembarked to survey the land. They traded goods with the natives and eventually took word of their discovery back to the Netherlands. In 1624, through violence and heavy-handed negotiation, the island of Mannahatta become a Dutch settlement. The first draft of modern Manhattan, whose forest traffic was already jammed with beavers and seagulls, was called New Amsterdam.

New York, I love you but you're bringing me down.

It was storming at midnight in August 2012 when my plane touched down at LaGuardia Airport. *Here goes nothing*, I thought. Holding everything I owned in my hands—two suitcases, one carry-on, one blanket, one pillow—I looked across the East River at the Manhattan skyline. The city was an imposing sea of black buildings speckled with ripples of light from inside windows. The rain added a reflective sheen to the dark skyline, resembling black leather or snake skin. The scene was stubbornly classic, like a vintage postcard or Woody Allen movie, but the city's imposing stature, authoritative and cold, made me feel as insignificant as a twig in Central Park. *What am I doing here?* I thought, waiting for a Brooklyn-bound cab. There is nothing as liberating and terrifying as a one-way airplane ticket. I was next in the taxi line. Rain hit my face as I let the view of Manhattan imprint my memory another second before opening the cab door. "Welcome back," the driver barked, and we were off.

Before boarding the plane to New York, I had given up one life—my job, my relationship, my apartment, boxes of junk I had accumulated over 10 years in Minneapolis—in exchange for the hope of another. All I had to my name was $3,000, an inconsistent résumé, a New York City MetroCard, and the lightness of letting go.

We are held down by what we hold on to. Over time, our attachments—whether mental, physical, or emotional—come to define us. And if we are not careful, we can become dependent on them. But what happens when a belief is proven false? What happens when an emotion is out of reach? What happens when possessions go away? Attachments feel comfortable but they can never provide lasting happiness. So there is freedom in letting go. The more baggage we release, the more value we find in what remains.

As soon as I arrived in New York, I attacked the job market, hoping my advertising experience would be a perfect fit for Madison Avenue. "Not so fast," the city said. "Advertising experience in Minnesota is one thing. Working in New York City is quite another. You're in the major leagues now, kid." Weeks passed and I remained unemployed as my savings dwindled away. Six weeks after my arrival, I finally received a call from the CEO of a tech start-up offering me a job. Graciously, I accepted, and my fear of starving to death dissipated.

Three days later I received another call from the CEO. "Hi James," he said. "Listen, I'm calling about your job offer. I hate to tell you this, but our company has lost an important financial investor. This happens with start-ups. I'm afraid we are unable to increase our staff as planned. Sorry about the turn of events, and good luck with your next opportunity."

I hung up the phone devastated. *Congratulations,* I said to myself. *You managed to get fired before even starting the job.* It was a new personal record. At that moment, the last of my "moving to New York excitement" vanished and I felt the skyscrapers closing in on me. They say that New York City breaks you down in order to build you back up. I was trying to build a new life in the city, but my resolve was breaking. I closed my MacBook and closed my eyes. *Show me what to do*, I thought to no one in particular.

Paradise lost.

From the moment Henry Hudson disembarked his ship, New York City was defined by conflict. The Dutch and Lenapes had opposing interests (the natives wanted to preserve the land, the Europeans to settle it), and tension was inevitable. Both groups initially benefited from a trading relationship, but harmony was severed when the immigrants claimed ownership of the land for the Dutch Republic. War ensued. The Dutch built a wooden wall across the southern end of the island, from one river to the other, to protect their settlement from Lenape attack. The street that ran along the wall was named Wall Street, a name still synonymous with protecting the interests of a privileged few.

The wall mitigated the Lenape threat and protected the Dutch, but there was no wall protecting the western shoreline when the British sailed into the harbor, weapons raised, in the summer of 1664. The Dutch were unprepared for the attack and signed control of the island over to the British without a fight. New Amsterdam was renamed New York to honor the king's little brother, the Duke of York.

But the Dutch did not go gently into the night. Nine years later, the Netherlands sent a fleet of 21 warships to reclaim the city, and the British were soundly defeated. The city's name changed again—from New York to New Orange. New Orange, alas, was not to be. The following year, Great Britain attacked again and regained ownership of the island, changing the name back to New York, this time for good. Great Britain ruled over New York City until 1783, when George Washington left his

Greenwich Village headquarters and rode his horse south to Fraunces Tavern on Pearl Street to tell the officers of the Continental Army in a teary-eyed speech that, since America had declared victory in the Revolutionary War, he would be resigning and returning to civilian life. New York City, and the United States of America, were now independent. But the young city, once teeming with wildlife and untapped potential, had blood on its hands. Innocence was traded like a beaver pelt for cash.

Moloch in whom I sit lonely.

Mo·loch
n.
In the Bible, the god of the Canaanites and Phoenicians to whom children were sacrificed.
A tyrannical power to be propitiated by human subservience or sacrifice; *"the great Moloch of war"*; *"duty has become the Moloch of modern life"*
— Norman Douglas
In Allen Ginsberg's poem "Howl," a metaphor for New York City: *"Moloch whose love is endless oil and stone! Moloch whose soul is electricity and banks! Moloch whose poverty is the specter of genius! Moloch whose fate is a cloud of sexless hydrogen! Moloch whose name is the Mind! Moloch in whom I sit lonely!"*

New York is a tough town. From Chinese immigrants of the 18th century, to Irish settlers escaping the great famine of the 19th Century, to thousands of annual transplants today who exchange their homes for cheap pizza and a chance to attain the mythical American Dream, newcomers are faced with trials and tribulations that challenge their commitment to keep up with the city that never sleeps. Pass the test and you are welcome to stay. Can't take the heat? You should leave Hell's Kitchen. If we are to make it—not just survive, but make it—the question we must ask ourselves is where we fit into this cacophony. How can we find our place among the discord?

When we practice mindfulness and retain a neutral state of mind, instead of allowing our thoughts to blow like garbage in a windy street, we remain peaceful even in the rat race.

From around the world, people keep coming, as though summoned by the same siren. New York is not one city; it is many, a spectrum that encompasses the wretched, the beautiful, the divine, and everything in between. Her streets symbolize our shared struggle and shared achievement. You will find God and the devil on the same sidewalk. Because New York is so many things at once, the city gives back whatever energy we bring to the table. The reality we experience is a reflection of our inner consciousness. Protecting our consciousness is therefore imperative. If we are not careful, the city can be a vacuum that drains our energy like a pickpocket. But when we practice mindfulness and retain a neutral state of mind, instead of allowing our thoughts to blow like garbage in a windy street, we remain peaceful even in the rat race. A cluttered mind is easily swept away. A steady mind parts the raging wind.

Our Ego tries to overcome the city's stress by fighting back against the tide of chaos and tangled agendas. This, of course, is impossible. We cannot use force to combat stress. Fighting with force only brings more force against us. Instead of waging war against the city, we must surrender the war within ourselves. This does not mean giving up our goals; it means giving up our Ego. There are two ways to engage life—with force or with flow. When we engage with force, the city fights back and rips our heart out. When we engage with flow, the city flows with us. The battle is won or lost before it begins.

If I can be mindful here, I can be mindful anywhere.

Living in a city is a spiritual test. The voices are many and the demands are urgent. "Do this. Buy that. Listen to me." The city is full of distractions pushing and pulling us in every direction. Our attention is our power. When we command our attention, we command our power. When we lose our attention, we lose our power. Commanding our own attention within the demanding city environment requires practice, patience, and forgiveness. Mindfulness is a muscle; when exercised, it grows. The city is the pressure that—when we pay attention to our thoughts—helps mindfulness grow stronger.

10 ways to stay mindful in the city (even on the subway).

1. Don't walk so fast. Nothing is as urgent as you think.

2. Forgive rude people. They are only protecting themselves.

3. Dedicate yourself to what you love and ignore everything else.

4. Be the eye of the storm. Project light and refuse to absorb darkness.

5. Respect the customs of the city even if you don't understand them. You are a guest in a home that has been here much longer than you.

6. Remain curious. Always explore.

7. Control the small things. Make your bed every morning, meditate every night, eat healthy, and spend time with people who make you better.

8. Make kindness a habit. What you do for others comes back.

9. Choose your own narrative. Remember that both happiness and stress are stories you tell yourself.

10. Always breathe deeply.

All of the lights.

As the sun set on Henry Hudson's crew on their first night in Mannahatta, they set up camp along the river and lit candles made from animal fat and strips of linen. They were the first candles to burn on the island, and in the centuries to come the city would seldom see darkness. The first street lamps, made from burning whale oil, were erected along the Bowery in the 1700s, illuminating the streets like never before. The entire city blazed with horror during the great New York City fires—first in 1776, and again in 1835. Thomas Edison started the Edison Electric Light Company (now called GE) in 1878 in order to sell his latest invention, the world's first commercially successful incandescent light bulb. By 1902, the Broadway theater district was nicknamed "the Great White Way" in honor of the glowing electric advertisements that stood as testament to the commercial spectacle of the city. In 2013, the Rockefeller Center Christmas tree, in a display fit for Santa Claus himself, delighted the Midtown tourists by flipping the switch on a record-breaking 45,000 multicolored LED bulbs.

Alluring lights have attracted visitors for centuries. We flutter like moths to a flame and lose ourselves in the glow. The brighter the light, the more readily we surrender our attention. Our primordial antenna buzzes, forgotten memories are triggered, and we seek momentary salvation in the artificial radiance. But salvation never comes. It cannot come because the illumination of the city, and in fact the splendor of the external world, however magnificent, is a counterfeit distraction from the light within ourselves. Just as our focus is distracted by the city, our inner compass is distracted by the flickering push and pull of the Ego. But we are not the Ego. We are more than passive observers of events beyond our control. We are creators of true light.

"The world is brighter and more powerful than me," the Ego says. "I wish I could be peaceful and happy, but life around me is too crazy."

"The light of the world is an illusion," the Higher Self says. "Your mind is the light that projects the image onto the screen. The world is merely the screen that displays your projection. You cannot change what is happening on the screen, but you can change the image you project. Outer reality is a projection of inner reality. Don't worry about changing the world; instead, change your focus. All places are filled with light. When you shine light on the darkness within yourself, the light around you becomes visible."

I turned off the lights and closed my eyes. Outside my apartment I heard the Brooklyn traffic howl like a hungry dog. Two months had passed in New York City and I was still unemployed. I opened my eyes and looked outside the window. Across the East River I could see the Statue of Liberty. From the distance it resembled a tourist replica. Earlier that night, the news gave warning that a hurricane was approaching. If the hurricane continued its trajectory, the weatherman said, it would be the most catastrophic storm in the city's history. I lay awake in bed with the lights off. Seeing nothing, I turned my attention within myself. *Inhale. Exhale. Inhale. Exhale.* For a brief moment I suspended my fear of the unknown and decided to accept, and even trust, uncertainty.

PART TWO

CULEBRA II:
THE WAR WITHIN

"The world problem is the individual problem; if the individual is at peace, has Happiness, has great tolerance, and an intense desire to help, then the world problem as such ceases to exist. You consider the world problem before you have considered your own problem. Before you have established peace and understanding in your own hearts and in your own minds, you desire to establish peace and tranquillity in the minds of others, in your nations and in your states; whereas peace and understanding will only come when there is understanding, certainty and strength in yourselves."

— JIDDU KRISHNAMURTI

Accding to legend, Christopher Columbus was the first European to set foot on Culebra. The year was 1493 and Columbus had embarked on his second Spanish-sanctioned voyage to the new world. The indigenous Caribs in Puerto Rico and Culebra, after whom the Caribbean was named, were not greeted kindly by the Spanish explorers. Many were murdered, others were enslaved. The brutal colonization of the West Indian Islands was underway.

This was not the first time Culebra had been invaded. Long before Christopher Columbus was born, the Caribs had attacked and overthrown—and, according to some accounts, cannibalized—the original inhabitants of the island, the Igneri, a people whose culture remains only in legend. Ownership of the island has changed hands many times since, and has often been leveraged as a bargaining chip by imperial nations. When the Spanish ceded control of Culebra to the United States as part of the Spanish-American War in 1898, nothing changed. One absentee landlord was replaced by another. The rolling hills, brilliant beaches, and wildlife diversity were left untouched by the United States until 1939, when the U.S. Navy turned the island into a bomb and artillery testing site. Over the next 35 years, warfare was tested and perfected on Culebra. Bombs rained from the sky and the white sand was tattooed with tank tread.

Under pressure from locals, the U.S. Navy ended bombing and gunnery operations in 1975. The tanks, planes, and bombs were removed from the island. Except one. One solitary tank remains, gathering rust on the rising shoreline of Flamenco Beach, a relic of American war games, eerily juxtaposed against the crisp blue sky.

Waving the white flag.

Sitting on Flamenco Beach, I observed the war within my mind between my Ego and my Higher Self as though I was moderating a debate between two politicians. The debate was tiresome, so I closed my eyes and stopped thinking. After what seemed like an hour, I opened my eyes and noticed an abandoned tank just down the beach from where I sat. The water had risen since 1975, when the U.S. Navy had abandoned Culebra, and the tank was sitting in shallow water. The words *love* and *peace* had been painted boldly on the tank's side. I contemplated the nature of war.

The human mind, when left to its own devices, exists in a state of turmoil. On one hand, we are channels of divine imagination and creativity. On the other hand, we are frightened animals desperate to survive. This conflict within ourselves, I realized, between angel and animal, is responsible for our state of global affairs. Ours is a world of parallel perfection and pain. The angel within us will rise, only to be pulled back into the swamp by our lower impulses. The animal will also rise, but scorched by the sun will soon retreat. During this battle we are unable to find peace within ourselves or with others. This is true on a small scale—with friends, families, and co-workers—and also on a large scale in politics, corporations, and nations. The history of war is the history of internal spiritual conflict.

As far back as records exist, war has been waged on earth. Every generation has seen differences of opinion between a few escalate into widespread terror and bloodshed. The clash of Egos has torn apart families and nations, severed us from our true nature, and left behind an aftermath of shock. The external impact is devastating, but every battle has an internal origin. The first war we face is inside ourselves. War is impossible when the mind is at peace.

Looking at my iPhone, I noticed it was afternoon. I was hungry and remembered that I had not eaten all day. All I had consumed had been wine. I thought about my conflicts with others over the years. I had been fired from jobs, fought with girlfriends, stepped over others to achieve success in my career, and survived occasional whiskey-fueled arguments during last call in Minneapolis dive bars like CC Club and Triple Rock. *What did these conflicts have in common?* I asked myself. The answer was that I had been living with unexamined conflict inside my mind, and my unchecked Ego was manifesting as conflict with others.

"I need to fight," the Ego says. "If I don't fight, I will be defeated."

"You cannot conquer your problems through conflict," the Higher Self says. "When you heal yourself, your problems—and your relationships—will also heal. The illusions of your Ego must be sacrificed at the altar of truth. A mind that is healed of conflict is like a world united under the banner of peace. It thinks and acts as one, without contradiction or division, and each thought serves a single purpose. The Ego cannot unite the mind, just as the Ego cannot unite the world. Surrender is not an act of defeat. It is an act of forgiveness. Only forgiveness can unite the mind, and only forgiveness can unite the world."

I listened to my thoughts and realized that the first step to creating peace and happiness in my life was resolving the conflict inside my mind. My Ego told me to be afraid and resist the present moment, but I listened with non-attachment and allowed my Ego's words to exist without identifying with them. I sat in meditation, paying attention to the quiet space between my thoughts, and before long the fear and conflict of my Ego seemed absurd. The ocean tide rose and fell. I chose to forgive myself for my fear and my failures. I gave up the fight.

A GUIDE TO
"BULLSH#T"
BY JAMES McCRAE

1. Opinion without principle.

2. Rules without purpose.

3. Tradition without flexibility.

4. Wealth without conscience.

5. Complaint without action.

6. Leadership without vision.

7. Work without passion.

CHAPTER 14

I'LL NEVER GET THERE

his is it. You are reading it now. *Sh#t Your Ego Says* is my first published book. And I will be honest. Finishing a book is not as easy as I hoped it would be when I wrote the first sentence. This is not to say I expected it to be a cakewalk, but I never expected it to feel so much like a plank walk. It's easy to start a book, they say, but hard to finish one. The hard part, it turns out, is not the writing. The hard part is sitting down every day, looking into the abyss of an empty Google Doc, and coming to terms with the cold stare of uncertainty and self-doubt. When I begin writing something, I have no clue what—if anything—will be written next.

Writing is an exercise in trust. The writer begins, and digs himself into a hole, at which point he becomes hopelessly stuck. Then he has a choice. He can either stop writing and walk away, or he can use words to dig his way out of the hole. Every morning when he sits down to write, he must dig another hole. And he must escape from it.

The size of the hole and the method of escape are different for every writer, but everyone faces the same uncertainty. And yet, the writing must begin. Pulled from the abyss of the blank screen, before the ending can be seen, the writing must begin. Sometimes I start with a story and hope the plot reveals a meaningful takeaway. Sometimes I start with a flash of inspiration and try to recall a story from my life that articulates the lesson. Sometimes I use my notebook to provoke my Ego, and pick my mental scabs to expose my wounds to the light, and hope like hell to make it out alive. Sometimes I gaze aimlessly into Google Docs with no idea what I will write and listen to the sound of silence until an idea accidentally smacks me in the face.

There are a million ways to write and it does not matter which way you choose. All that matters is that you start. Once you start, the door cracks open, slowly at first, and before long the mystery is revealed. Don't worry about getting lost. If your work is good, you are guaranteed to get lost. Give yourself space to wander. Wandering leads to wondering, and wondering leads to revelation. Keep clawing further into the hole you have dug until you see a crack of light. When I begin writing a new chapter, like this one, I cannot see the finish line. But I trust that the finish line is there. And it is. Even when I get lost along the way, I always find it.

Today's focus is tomorrow's reality.

Living a life with purpose is similar to writing. When we decide to stop following the status quo and start living according to our higher truth, there is no blueprint. The future is a blank page, and the life we envision may seem far away, blurry, and even impossible. And yet, like the first step of a marathon, we must start the race before the finish line is visible. This is daunting because the Ego is afraid of what it cannot see. "What if I fail?" the Ego asks. "What if I am not smart or talented enough?" In spite of these concerns, in writing and life, we must choose to disregard the possibility of failure, say "Fuck it," and begin anyway. Where we focus today, before results can be seen, determines our reality tomorrow.

Don't worry about getting lost. If your work
is good, you are guaranteed to get lost.
Give yourself space to wander.
Wandering leads to wondering,
and wondering leads to revelation.

There is always a way. No forest is too thick and no market
is too crowded. But no one can show us the way. We must pave
the path to our purpose ourselves. This is not as impossible as
it sounds. Think about it. Deep down, we all have a sense of
destiny calling to us. We may not believe we can hear it, but
we can. To realize consciously what we already know subconsciously, we simply must listen. When we quiet the mind and
trust our intuition, our destiny, and the path to realizing it,
become clear.

"My dreams are too far away," the Ego says. "What if I
never get there?"

"When you begin a journey, you will often doubt that you
are on the correct path," the Higher Self says. "The road map
may be unclear—at first, it usually is—but that's okay. Fear is
an indication that you are relying on the power of the Ego. Confidence—not Ego cockiness, but steadfast inner strength—is an
indication that you are relying on the power of divine guidance.
Others may doubt you, and at times you may doubt yourself.
But doubt is a self-imposed speed limit. The finish line reveals
itself according to the degree of your commitment. Don't worry
about how. Just believe."

Our dreams are not an accident. What we are capable of
dreaming we are capable of being. We all have a vision that
sees beyond our intelligence. We feel a magnetic pull toward
something beyond ourselves. This is the territory we are

being called to explore. "I'll never get there," the Ego says. And therefore it will not. Beliefs are a self-fulfilling prophecy. Believe you will get there or believe you will not. Either way you are right.

CHAPTER 15

PROFIT OVER PURPOSE

Change usually comes when we least expect it, like a surprise pregnancy or a car crash where two unaware drivers are inexplicably bound by a shared cosmic fate. Plan as we may, it is the unforeseen moments—like turning the corner and locking eyes with a stranger who will change our lives forever—that carry more significance than a decade of planned routine. This is how I felt one summer afternoon after receiving an unexpected job offer.

Working in advertising is like being in an open relationship; one is only as faithful as one's options. Résumés are exchanged like the common cold. The industry appears to be a ladder, but more accurately resembles a hamster wheel. Everyone is reaching for the next rung—a better position, a better agency, better clients—but secretly wondering exactly where, if anywhere, they are going. I was no different. Like most of my agency comrades, I felt overworked and underpaid, and was always looking out for a more attractive rung on the ladder. One summer in particular, fed up with my job, I shared my résumé more aggressively than usual.

It had been more than one year since I had returned to New York from Culebra, and in order to support myself I was once again working as a strategist for a creative agency. While my time in Culebra had evolved my thinking in many ways, my Ego had not gone away completely, and I was experiencing bouts of frustration. The Ego, I was beginning to realize, dies a slow death, and even great inspiration requires practice to maintain.

Nearly every agency in New York City heard from me over the course of three weeks. There was nothing I could do but wait. And nothing happened. Not even an interview. Days turned into weeks. Then came the e-mail.

It was a recruiter named Sue Baker, and she wanted to schedule me for a job interview. *Strange,* I thought. *I don't remember applying for this job.* And I hadn't. After applying to dozens of jobs, spending hours on LinkedIn, and receiving zero responses, I was being recruited out of the blue for an even better position than those I had been pursuing. It was not until the end of the message, when I saw Sue's e-mail signature, that I noticed the name of the company. I gasped. It was a corporate agency infamous for its work with, among other questionable clients, cigarette companies.

After much hesitation, I decided to take the interview. While I did not like the idea of working for a cigarette company, I did like the idea of earning more money. *Besides,* I thought. *How bad could it be?* One week later I arrived for the interview. The summer day's sunny mood shifted when I exited the elevator on the 33rd floor. The lights in the office were dim and there was a distinct absence of fresh air. The employees wore suits and nobody made eye contact. After 10 minutes I was led by the receptionist to a conference room and asked to sit down at the largest marble table I had ever seen. Across from me sat four marketing directors, men in their mid-40s with broad shoulders and slick hair. Three wore black suits. One wore a gray suit. They looked like mirror images of each other. I was not a smoker, but suddenly I wanted a cigarette.

They fired questions like bullets. Most questions were related to my work experience, but they also asked about my willingness to embrace their corporate culture. "This is the kind of place," one marketing director said, "where we have your back if you have ours. The company is a ladder. If you play your cards right you can reach the top. If your allegiance is strong, I promise, you can have it all." The marketing director crossed his legs and grinned. It was the first smile I had seen all day.

The interview lasted one hour but felt longer. *Okay, the vibe in that office was definitely not good,* I thought in the taxi going home. We weaved around Park Avenue toward my uptown apartment. *But then again,* I considered, *business is about success, not good vibes.* My Ego wanted me to take the job—after all, my lifestyle and tax bracket would improve—but my Higher Self had doubts. I could not decide whether my career should be measured by outward appearance or inner purpose. The taxi approached 42nd Street and we drove up the Park Avenue Viaduct and turned right at Grand Central Terminal. I wondered how many suits I would need to buy if I took the job.

The most important choice of your career.

Here's the thing. We actually can, as the marketing director said, have it all. In fact, there are two ways to have it all. The two ways are very different, but both require our full dedication. Whichever way we choose will cause a domino effect of changes across our lives, and will impact our happiness, our relationships, and—perhaps most importantly—our ability to have a good night's sleep. Both ways will change our lives forever.

Society is making us an offer. If we accept this offer, society promises to take care of us. The offer is simple: Follow the rules, fit in, keep our opinions to ourselves, and work diligently to support the interests of the establishment. If our allegiance is strong, society says, our needs will be met. But there is a catch. In return, we must surrender our dreams, our purpose, and anything else that does not serve the agenda of the status quo.

The purpose of life is not to obtain the outward appearance of success. The purpose of life is to excavate and actualize our personal truth.

Luckily there is another offer on the table. Again there is much to surrender. The second offer requires that we forsake our fear and reactionary thinking in exchange for complete trust in the universe to fulfill our needs. This includes releasing the desire for money, success, and recognition—which often become comfortable states of mind, like a crutch—and exchanging the limiting belief of personal lack for the expansive belief of personal abundance. As part of this deal, we must agree to respond to all circumstances with love, understanding that an attitude of acceptance will create space for the necessary events to unfold in our lives.

In other words, we can achieve the desires of our Ego, as long as we sacrifice our dreams and purpose. Or we can attain inner fulfillment, and step into a higher version of ourselves, as long as we eradicate the fear and desire of the Ego. This is the most important choice of our career.

Truth comes to light.

Truth is built to last. What is fake soon fades. The pursuit of profit over purpose is a result of Ego conditioning that will eventually be exposed to light. The purpose of life is not to obtain the outward appearance of success. The purpose of life is to excavate and actualize our personal truth. Does that sound like a lot of pressure? It's not. The day we begin living our truth, the pressure goes away because we are no longer hiding behind the expectations and standards of others. We can stop acting and simply be ourselves.

It was only a job, but it felt like more. It felt like I was choosing a path that would define the future of my life and career. The money was tempting. But I didn't like the idea of who I might become. After two nights of meditation, I decided that success should be measured not by résumé credentials, but rather by the degree to which I felt connected to my higher purpose. Vibes matter. And the vibes of the job did not feel right. I never called them back.

Peace of mind is more important than money, and I trusted that by remaining true to myself, the money would be provided in the right place at the right time. I continued showing up for my old job. But I had a renewed sense of freedom. From that day forward I understood that purpose is more valuable than profit. That simple truth has guided my career since. I may not have it all, but it feels like I do.

nothing
exists

except: ~~mdd~~
1) vibration
2) empty space

everything
else is
opinion.

CHAPTER 16

I WANT TO BE FAMOUS

rowing up, I had more friends than I could count, thousands of them. They came in all shapes and sizes—fast friends, slow friends, funny friends, smart friends, awkward friends, rebellious friends, spiritual friends, and downright troublemakers. Together we had great adventures. I'm not talking about other kids. I'm talking about words—letters that formed sentences strung together as paragraphs that found their home in poems and books. They were my constant companions, and we got along famously. Sure, I made time for other hobbies—playing sports, watching television, fishing, boyhood mischief—but my favorite pastime was, letter by letter, crafting words, and fusing those words into sentences, and introducing one sentence to another to see how they got along. I was, and still am, fascinated by the pen's alchemic ability to transfer imagination onto paper and document the unseen. I could reach into my mind and pull out anything I wanted. It was magic, plain and simple.

I kept my words to myself. They say the best way to love is without attachment, and my friendship with words had no expectations or hidden agenda. We shared openly because words did not expect me to be anyone I was not, and I did not expect words to be anyone they were not. Our understanding was mutual. If words were shy, I did not pressure them. When they arrived with enthusiasm, I was ready to play. I did not use words to reach an outcome. They did not use me. We loved without attachment until our relationship fell apart.

When the breakdown began, exactly, I cannot say, but it was my fault. In my 20s, as my desire for success grew, my motivation changed. Instead of writing without attachment, and appreciating the joy of each word as it came, I began writing with the agenda of receiving recognition for my work. A few people, mostly friends and family members, had complimented my writing. I liked the feeling of validation. It felt good to be praised and, like an addict who chases the dragon of their first hit, over time I began chasing recognition.

My creativity suffered. Instead of writing, as I had in the past, about things that mattered to me, I began submitting articles to popular websites and magazines for the sole purpose of getting attention. My style also changed. My tone became cynical and judgmental because I believed that sarcasm would make my writing more popular. The more I chased validation from others, the less satisfaction I felt within myself. My relationship with writing had been spoiled. Words were no longer magic; they were cheap.

The fame delusion.

To the Ego, nothing is more important than being important. Sure, everyone likes to feel validation. Our community is our tribe, and validation gives us a sense of belonging and contribution to our tribe. But validation can be addictive. If we are not careful, we can start measuring our happiness by the approval we receive from the world. This is one of the Ego's favorite tricks. Unable to find satisfaction and wholeness within itself, the Ego will claw on the doors of others until it receives the attention it craves. The problem is that whatever we chase, especially from a place of neediness, becomes more difficult to attain. The more we rely on approval from others to find happiness, the more we disconnect from our inner ability to create happiness for ourselves. And all lasting happiness is homemade.

Greatness cannot be obtained; it is already within us. We simply must strip away the Ego and stand naked in our power.

"Fame will make me happy," the Ego says. But I worked in advertising long enough to understand that fame is not real. The concept of celebrity is an illusion. The people we see, and aspire to become, in television, magazines, and movies, are not real people. They are manufactured archetypes designed to pull the emotional heartstrings of audience demographics. We have the temptress, the rebel, the hero, the lover, the girl next door, and more. Each of these archetypes is appealing because advertising is designed to mirror our psychological desires and stimulate brain activity. But the truth is that the people behind the retouched image of celebrity perfection are as conflicted, flawed, awkward, and vulnerable as anybody else. When we pull away the curtain we can see that fame is merely a staged product placement designed to drive desire and revenue. Yet the idea of fame is something that many people continue to chase. The rise of the omnipresent media culture has increased our opportunity, and therefore our appetite, for celebrity status. We pursue fame because it promises outward love to compensate for inner lack—which, of course, is impossible—and this reflects our society's inability to generate happiness from within.

Greatness cannot be obtained; it is already within us. We simply must strip away the Ego and stand naked in our power.

Your only job is to speak your truth.

"I exist as I am, that is enough,
If no other in the world be aware I sit content,
And if each and all be aware I sit content."

— WALT WHITMAN

I gave the story a final edit and sent the e-mail. It had taken me nearly a month to write, but my article for a major online magazine was finally submitted. This milestone should have called for champagne, but I wanted a nap. My Ego was pleased but my emotions were depleted, and I did not know why. I can see now that I had forgotten a basic truth. When we work with a sense of purpose, the energy we put into our work will be recycled back to us. But when our actions are not natural, and we attempt to force an outcome, our energy will shrivel and fade.

My motivation for writing the story was unnatural. I wanted desperately to be published. I wanted attention. I wanted more Twitter followers. And, believing it would make me more popular, I wrote in a cynical voice that was not true to myself. My motivation was not authentic so my writing was not authentic. It was a shallow grab for attention to compensate for the voice inside me telling me that I was not good enough. The article was never published.

"I work hard," the Ego says. "And I deserve recognition for my work."

"We live in a world that is starving for truth," the Higher Self says. "Recognition, therefore, does not come from chasing validation; it comes from expressing your authentic self. In our cultural marketplace, individuality is worth more than conformity. One voice that sings from the heart carries more power than a choir straining to hit notes they do not believe in.

Recognition does not come from molding yourself according to the world's definition of success, but rather from shining the light of your unique perspective."

"But what if I express my authentic self and nobody listens?" the Ego says.

The purpose of listening to a musical composition is not to reach the end. The purpose is to enjoy the flow of the music. Life is the same way. Lasting happiness means finding renewed joy in each passing moment.

"Your only job is to speak your truth," the Higher Self says. "Upon birth everyone alive was given a candle. This candle is your truth. Your job is to protect your candle and keep the flame alive. It does not matter how many people see your candle or how big the light grows. The only thing that matters is that your flame always burns. The people who will benefit from your light will find you. You may wish you had a bigger candle, or you will be tempted to abandon your candle so you can bask in the light of another's. But, when you allow your truth to shine, everything you need is already within the flame of the candle you were given."

"But the reason I want to be famous," the Ego says, "is because fame will make me happy."

"Happiness is a paradox," the Higher Self says. "Before you can receive it from others, you must have it within yourself. You have convinced yourself that a barrier exists between you and happiness. But happiness is available every moment. The only obstacle is your belief that you do not deserve to be happy. When the curtain of your Ego is pulled away, happiness is revealed as your birthright and natural state of being."

Happiness is a wild animal.

It was not until years later, after realizing that chasing fame is a dead end, that I fixed my relationship with writing. I remembered why I had fallen in love with words in the first place. It had nothing to do with attention, and everything to do with the witchcraft of pulling a coded sequence of letters from the sky and merging them together to riff on some universal truth filtered through my personal perspective.

When I started writing *Sh#t Your Ego Says*, a lot of people gave me feedback. "You should find an agent," they said. "You should focus on growing your social media followers. Your writing is not as important as your marketing platform." In spite of popular opinion and pressure from publishers, I politely disagreed. I had been down that road before, and I knew that if my objective was solely to obtain mass exposure, then my words, and my message, would be compromised. Our words are our truth, and our truth is our candle. The impact of our vision is stronger when we commit to protecting our flame.

I once believed that fame would make me happy. But happiness is a wild animal. As soon as we try to catch it, it evades us. Instead of caging happiness, what if we ran wild alongside it and howled at the wind for no reason, greeting each passing moment, without neediness or expectation, as an open door? The magic is alive during the process, not embalmed in the tomb of results. Every morning when I sit down to write, I write with the intention of discovering something new within myself, something knocking that I have been too busy to hear.

The joy is the discovery. The result might be (and might not be) popular, but that is not an outcome I am attached to. The purpose of listening to a musical composition is not to reach the end. The purpose is to enjoy the flow of the music. Life is the same way. Lasting happiness means finding renewed joy in each passing moment.

CHAPTER 17

CONTROL PEOPLE

There was once a powerful CEO. He was nearing retirement and it was time to choose a successor. He called his two sons into his office to announce his decision to bestow control of the company to one of them. "My boys," the CEO said. "One of you will soon be given a great responsibility. Running this company is a great joy and a great duty. Your leadership will determine the success of the company and the happiness of our employees, so please spend the next few days considering the type of leader you plan to be."

The older son's eyes lit up with excitement. *This is a great opportunity*, he thought. *I will have power over the company and our employees. It is best to manage with strength and discipline, and allow nothing to fall outside my control. I need to demonstrate my power and instill the fear of failure into the hearts of our employees.*

The younger son was also excited. *This is an important responsibility*, he thought. *Our employees will count on me for leadership. The decisions I make will affect thousands of lives. If I invest love into my employees, they will invest love into their work. I hope I am ready to be a wise leader. If we are to succeed, I must empower my employees to fulfill their highest potential.*

"Remember that power has no inherent value," the CEO said. "Power can be a tool for good or evil, depending on the values of those in power. Your values will have a tremendous impact on others, so choose your values wisely."

Finally, the older son thought. *I can control others.*

Finally, the younger son thought. *I can set others free.*

How do you use your power?

Most of us will never be the CEO of a large corporation, but everyone has power. You may have power in your career, your family, or your social circle. Maybe you have children. Maybe there is somebody who looks up to you. Even small actions have power because everyone is connected through the web of human relationships. How we use our power, whether big or small, has an impact that returns to us. Power, even great power, is never one-sided. Power is a relationship. Every action toward another is an action toward ourselves. So whether we are a CEO or a dishwasher, a universal truth remains: those who limit others, limit themselves; those who empower others, empower themselves.

"I want to control people," the Ego says. "You and I are in opposition because we are separate from each other. Resources are limited and only one of us can win. My guard must remain up. I need to control others to avoid being controlled."

"The universe is not a race," the Higher Self says. "The concept of winners and losers is an outdated model of thinking. Everyone is connected, and what benefits you also benefits another. When you trust and empower others, their actions will be inspired. Therefore great leaders use their power to create an environment that allows each person to act from a place of personal purpose."

Which son are you?

One week later the CEO called his sons into his office. "I have decided to remain in control of the company for three years," he said. "After three years I will retire and one of you will assume the title of CEO. I look forward to choosing whoever is most prepared."

This is bad, the older son thought. *My father should recognize that he is too old and weak to continue running the company. I am ready to take control now.*

This is good, the younger son thought. *Now I can practice my leadership skills, and learn from my father, and in three years I will be more prepared to serve others.*

IN CASE OF
EMERGENCY
———————————
BREAK
ROUTINE

CHAPTER 18

FEAR THE UNKNOWN

here is something about a New Orleans night that turns accident into magic. New Orleans possesses an unorthodox rhythm—like the city's most famous export, jazz music—that permits freedom to anyone loose and open-eared enough to choose improvisation over convention and follow an impulse to its natural conclusion. If the city was a bandleader it would be a democratic one, deconstructing melodies like Ornette Coleman, allowing each player to riff upon their own tonal center. When rules are broken, there is an unexpected logic in the frenzy that follows. This is the town where Louis Armstrong was born, Tennessee Williams wrote, and Pete Maravich turned basketball into performance art. Highway 61, the central nervous system of American music, springs northward from the French Quarter, and for decades carried previously unheard stories and guitar chord progressions from the swampy bayou into the national spotlight. Tension dissipates here, like blue notes of bebop into muggy air, or a ghost finally ready to say good-bye.

It's no accident that the Mississippi River, heavy with emotional residue from America's heartland, passes through New Orleans before finally purging our sins into the redeeming Gulf of Mexico.

It was my first time in New Orleans and my friends wanted to get drunk. The bars were festive and the February air was warmer than I expected. A cold beer sounded good, but I had other plans.

"They let you drink in the streets here," Matt said. "It's only six o'clock. We should walk around the French Quarter and hit every bar. I can drink you all under the table."

Mardi Gras was two weeks away and the spirit was beginning to stir. A young man passed us wearing a purple bandana wrapped around his head. He played a brass trumpet and a beautiful woman with dark gypsy eyes followed behind him dancing to the rhythm of her own tambourine.

"Look," Matt said, pointing elsewhere. "It's the Cats Meow. They have awesome karaoke."

Laura smiled and rolled her eyes. She didn't say anything. She didn't have to. We both knew that the New Orleans we had come to find, a mysterious city steeped in legends both true and half-true, would not be found inside a karaoke bar. We followed our friends as they crossed the street toward Cats Meow.

"We'll meet you guys inside," I lied.

The sky was growing dark and the air was cooling. Laura and I walked past Cats Meow and continued walking. We moved quickly, holding hands, ducking and dodging tourists carrying cocktails in oversized cups. As we made our escape from Bourbon Street, Laura spotted a patch of yellow wildflowers growing alongside the cobblestone streets. She picked some and carefully placed them into the breast pocket of my jacket.

"There," she said. "Just like a high priest."

We rented vintage bikes and rode into the night looking for the ghost of New Orleans.

Destination unknown.

We rode north into Tremé. The scenic streets resembled a collision between a French kingdom and a third world nation.

Storybook mansions—pink, baby blue, and yellow—framed the dusty streets; their fading facades, withered with character, accentuated the stories they seemed to tell. Wildflowers grew behind rusted gates. Flags proudly hung from porches and windows displaying the local cultural iconography: fleurs-de-lis, Mardi Gras masks, the New Orleans Saints. The occasional rum bottle, empty or broken, could be found sleeping on the sidewalk, seemingly unaware that the sun had risen and the party was over. A wooden sign rose from the garden of a 19th-century Greek Revival mansion. "Be nice or go home," it read. This seemed to be the unofficial New Orleans motto. Everything felt imaginary.

We locked our bikes to a street sign and stepped into Louis Armstrong Park. The park, sweet and tuneful, was fit for the legacy of its namesake. And there he was. We approached a statue of the great trumpeter himself, Satchmo, icon and ambassador of American music, whose howling baritone had served as the soundtrack for many of our road trips and dinner parties. We asked a stranger to take our picture in front of the statue, and kissed while the sun set behind Satchmo's million-dollar smile. We wandered farther into the park and came upon a vast open space. The clearing was large, probably two acres in diameter, and dozens of trees were planted along the perimeter. The ground was embedded with stone tiles that flowered outward from the center in geometric patterns. We could tell there was something intentional, maybe even sacred, about this preservation of empty space. It was not a religious site, at least not in a traditional sense, but something told us to approach with caution.

This quiet space was called Congo Square, and the sacred nature of the site was, it turned out, intentional. Congo Square was an important meeting place for 18th-century slaves who congregated here to play music, sing African songs, and, most importantly, dance. It was one of the only places where early African Americans could practice and preserve the cultural traditions that were in danger of disappearing after the violent uprooting of West African villages during the Atlantic slave trade.

Many tribes gathered in Congo Square, including the Fon people, who originated in the African kingdom of Dahomey (modern day Benin) and arrived as slaves in the Southern U.S. and Caribbean islands. The Fon kept alive, to the best of their ability and often in secret, many Dahomey traditions. This flame tended would eventually, over the course of centuries, spread like wildfire into American culture, beyond what anyone could have imagined. Among the seeds that Dahomey descendants planted was the ritualistic union of music and dance to bridge the gap between the material and spiritual worlds. More than 200 years later, nearly all popular music in the Unites States—including jazz, rock 'n' roll, and hip-hop—can trace its origin to ceremonies in New Orleans and other Southern cities that joined rhythm and movement as part of tribal ritual.

Over time these ceremonies merged with local Catholic influences and morphed into a new religion, both celebratory and sacred, that linked African history with American society. They called the religion voodoo after the Fon word for spirit. Voodoo practices were joyful and the music was uplifting. With the vision of early leaders like Queen Marie Laveau, Louisiana voodoo arose from slave chambers into Congo Square and the streets of New Orleans and beyond.

African American traditions, beginning in places like Congo Square, have been so absorbed into our cultural vocabulary that our music, art, and language would be unrecognizable without their influence. What Laura and I did not realize was that some of these practices, including voodoo, were still practiced in New Orleans today, more or less in their original form.

The evening air was crisp. We exited Louis Armstrong Park and emerged on Rampart Street. We unlocked our bikes and walked them along the sidewalk without speaking. Laura stopped and pointed across the street to a wooden sign hanging from a storefront. We crossed the street to take a closer look. My graphic design education did nothing to help me decipher the cryptic iconography painted in red and black on the triangular sign.

The thin lines had a feminine quality, which was complemented by a crescent moon hanging above a triangle inside a circle with a slightly larger circumference. Inside the triangle was an abstract altar drawn from geometric shapes. The symmetry was broken on the right side by a snake reaching vertically toward the sky. The symbolism resembled lost hieroglyphics or a black-magic instruction manual. The neighboring buildings on Rampart Street were the type of gift shops one would expect to find on a popular street in a tourist town. But those buildings did not interest us. With curiosity—and more than a little trepidation—Laura and I opened the front door and walked into the New Orleans Voodoo Spiritual Temple.

Here we only practice the light.

Our friends are probably having a blast, I thought. By now, they had probably downed three or four shots of Jägermeister, and maybe scored coke in a bar, or smoked an alley joint with jazz musicians. Karaoke singers were certainly serenading the crowd from the Cats Meow stage, drunkenly croaking a perfect tune, at least to them. I was not above this scene, far from it. I had shared many restless nights with complete strangers turned best friends over a shared love for cheap beer, expensive whiskey, and the rambling piano of a Billy Joel ballad. Those nights, and the less glamorous mornings that followed, summarized the weekends of my 20s. I spent a decade collecting stress at work and throwing it down with reckless abandon at night. And I had the stories, the tattoos, and the angry ex-girlfriends to prove it.

But I was ready to make a change. It was a fun ride that had gotten me nowhere. Laura, my charming girlfriend whose red hair burned like the Southern sunset, possessed a free spirit that had followed her from San Francisco to New York City, and she felt the same way. It's not that we were rebellious. We did not want to break rules for the sake of being different. We simply believed that the meaning of life is discovered, not given, and we wanted to explore the parameters of convention to understand what was worth keeping, and what was not.

The first thing I noticed was the music. An eerie drum sound echoed from speakers inside the Voodoo Spiritual Temple, but seemed to be coming from another world. The compositional elements of the music were easy to identify—drums, vocals, gong, rattle, an occasional bass line—but the overall cadence resembled antique phrases that had long ago left the common lexicon but retained a phonetic impact that still resonated.

The second thing I noticed was a sign toward the back of the temple. "All traditions contain both light and dark elements," the sign read. "Here we only practice the light." We saw nobody. Shelves and tables were cluttered with relics, both sacred and tacky. A wooden totem of a woman with exaggerated breasts and ass was placed next to a collection of metal snakes. Charms and amulets called gris-gris (objects that ward off evil spirits) were sitting on a pile of spell books. Candles, incense, tarot cards, cloth dolls, paintings of Queen Marie Laveau, and prayer beads surrounded colorful plastic figurines of Jesus Christ and Mother Mary. I surveyed the animal skulls—real or not, I still do not know—sitting next to dreams catchers, beaded necklaces, and African masks, until my eyes finally settled on a photograph of the temple's proprietor, Priestess Miriam.

We had just entered, and already I wanted to leave. The room felt like holy ground on which I did not belong. In spite of my hesitation we stepped forward to explore the room. The walls were alive with the sensual aroma of death and mystery. The spirit was here—some spirit, somewhere—whose exact location could not be seen but whose fragrance penetrated the air like summer humidity. We were in it. The cypress trees in the swampland, layered with Spanish moss and guarded by herds of alligators, understood the mystery. So did the rising tide of Bayou St. John, where a passageway into another dimension was, legend says, opened in 1860 and never again closed. We were standing in the shade of such myths, surrounded by relics and symbols that represented the mortal bond with the angelic, and I was uneasy. That's when Priestess Miriam, with the unexpected scurry of a New Orleans crawfish, appeared from nowhere into the room.

The name Priestess Miriam sounded familiar but I could not remember why. Her reputation preceded her like a fairy tale. I assumed that she was either a commercial creation of New Orleans tourism or a legend of voodoo history like Queen Marie Laveau. But here she was, a real person, and she walked into the room with as generous a smile as you were likely to find outside the Louis Armstrong statue across the street. She wore a long, red scarf over a white dress, and her thick black hair pointed, like her personality, up.

I think I said hello but don't remember. I was too busy thinking that I should say hello to remember whether or not I actually said it. She smiled and I smiled back, but I quickly returned to observing the African masks on the wall, avoiding eye contact. What else does one do when meeting a famous voodoo priestess other than play it cool and look the other way? Laura and Miriam, however, had instant chemistry. They greeted each other warmly, and Miriam pointed out some of the temple's relics and explained their history. I did my best to listen, but Laura and Miriam were behaving like old friends, so I continued observing the heirlooms of the temple—stone crucifixes and photographs of Geronimo—and allowed girl talk to continue uninterrupted.

Together, Miriam and Laura radiated a gentle energy that glowed like embers from a Mardi Gras bonfire. They continued talking and moved from the public storefront into the back corridors of the temple. Miriam turned and gestured at me to follow, which I did at a distance, understanding that I was the third wheel of the group. I busied myself by taking photos with my iPhone, roaming from room to room in the dimly lit temple capturing scenes I was unlikely to see again.

After 15 minutes of wandering, I returned to the largest room of the temple, the altar room, where I had last seen the girls. Miriam was gone. My girlfriend was still there, writing in the notebook she carried everywhere. I took one last photograph of Laura. She was dimly lit by candles, her hair glowing as one with the altar behind her.

"Did you have a good conversation?" I asked.

"So good," she said.

"What did you talk about?"

Laura considered the question. "Miriam told me how she had discovered voodoo by accident as a young woman in Chicago. And she asked me what I wanted to do with my life. I told her that I was thinking of becoming a writer. Miriam laughed when I said that. She said that thoughts, like wishes, mean very little. Instead of thinking, she said we must know. And she gave me this."

Laura pulled a scrap of paper from her denim jacket pocket. Handwritten was a street address and three words: *Voodoo ceremony. Tonight.*

"Can we go?" Laura asked. I could hear in her voice that I was in no position to say no.

We left the temple and returned to our bikes to embark on another journey into the streets of New Orleans. I could not tell what it was, but something about Laura was different. She had magic in her eyes. I called her Priestess from that day forth.

No turning back.

"The cave you fear to enter holds the treasure that you seek."

— JOSEPH CAMPBELL

It was midnight when we arrived, and the stars above Rosalie Alley were crystal clear. I had no idea where we were.

The winding backstreets had taken us far from the familiarity of Rampart Street—past the dive bars, the tattoo shops, and families of stray cats and dogs—into an unlit residential neighborhood. It was a far cry from the Creole mansions on Bourbon Street, but the colorful homes and wooden fences decorated with dancing skeletons were unmistakably New Orleans.

There was nowhere to lock our bikes. We looked for a street sign, a pole, anything that could be used to secure our bikes with a U-shaped lock. There was nothing. Rather than turn around, we decided to leave our rented bikes unlocked against an oak tree in the middle of the block. We walked along the sidewalk looking for the correct street address.

"300. 302. 306," Laura said. "Where is 304?"

We stepped closer and noticed an unpaved walkway. After an unspoken hesitation, we tiptoed in unison off the sidewalk toward the passageway that resembled, more in ambiance than appearance, the mouth of a cave, and we stepped into Rosalie Alley. We stopped. We took another step and stopped.

"We should turn around," I whispered. "We're trespassing."

"Shhh," Laura cut me off. "Look."

There was a lamp hanging from the side of a shed that illuminated the walkway ahead and revealed the shapes of seven or eight people, not moving, dressed head to toe in white.

"Seriously," I whispered. "We are walking unannounced into an actual voodoo ceremony. We have no idea what to expect. This has been fun, but we should return to our bikes. They're not even locked."

Laura said nothing and reached out her hand to hold mine.

We approached them. They were quiet. The shed door was closed but inside we heard drumming and chanting. We waited. Nobody told us to leave, or questioned who we were, or said anything to us, so we stayed. An older black man nodded. We nodded back. All at once I felt both big and small, an eternity inside a grain of sand and a grain of sand inside eternity. The spirit was here—some spirit, somewhere—and I felt embarrassingly out of place.

"Induction ceremony," the man said, pointing to the shed. "When they are finished, we will go inside."

I waited for more information, but none was given, so I nodded again, acting natural. The drumming inside the shed continued, and I thought I heard somebody scream, but could not be certain.

Laura and I were dressed for New York City. She wore her vintage blue-denim jacket. I was wearing a black hat, black jeans, and a black jacket. The only pop of color came from the yellow wildflowers in my jacket pocket. Everybody else wore white, and we looked how we felt—out of place—but we were not the only two attending a voodoo ceremony for the first time.

"What do you know about voodoo?" I asked a young man with a spiked afro wearing a white Guns N' Roses T-shirt. His name was Andre. Like us, he had arrived in New Orleans the day before. Unlike us, his visit to Rosalie Alley was not accidental. He had flown by himself from Pittsburgh to New Orleans, searching for the crossroads where lightness and darkness collide.

"Not much," Andre admitted. "Only what I learned today at the Island of Salvation Botanica."

"Island of what?" I asked.

"Island of Salvation Botanica," Andre repeated. We both paused and Andre continued. "Last year on my birthday I received a package. It smelled like smoke and there was no return address. Inside the package was a deck of tarot cards designed by Sallie Ann Glassman. I had never heard of Sallie Ann Glassman before, but it turns out she is a modern leader, a torchbearer of sorts, in Haitian and New Orleans voodoo."

"Did you ever discover who sent the tarot cards?" I asked.

"No," he continued. "But I discovered that they were sold at the Island of Salvation Botanica, which is a store that Sallie Ann Glassman owns. The package terrified me because I had been having recurring dreams about tarot cards, although I had never used them and knew nothing about them. I tossed the cards in the trash. Exactly one year later, on my next birthday, I received another package. Same thing. It was another set of tarot cards from the Island of Salvation Botanica, again with no return address. This time I really freaked out. Who was sending me these cards? My dreams about tarot had returned too. The coincidence was too overwhelming to ignore. I took the first flight from Pittsburgh to New Orleans. That was yesterday."

My own story—sneaking away from Bourbon Street bar-hopping—paled in comparison, so I did my best to keep Andre talking. "The synchronicity of your story is remarkable," I said. "And what about Sallie Ann Glassman? Did you find her?"

Andre looked at me blankly. "Don't you know where we are?" he asked.

I shook my head. "Not really," I admitted.

"We're here," Andre said. "This is Sallie's property. This is her ceremony."

The shed doors swung open and the sound of the drumming increased. Candlelight and sage smoke poured from the entrance. The initiation, apparently, was complete, and we all looked up in anticipation. Dressed in white, turban wrapped around her brown hair, her eyes gentle, stood Sallie Ann Glassman, voodoo priestess and patron saint of the bayou. She wasted no time dispelling any notion of myth or superiority. Perhaps sensing our hesitation, she broke the heavy air with light laughter.

"Thank you for coming," she greeted us warmly. "Please come in."

The drumming paused. Laura and I allowed the rest of the group to enter and followed. Our intention, after all, was to be spies, not soldiers.

Our luck is only as good as our courage.

The shed was spacious and dark. Dozens of candles glowed, their light reflected by metal and glass objects placed in four or five elaborate altars around the room. The voodoo altar, I later learned, originated in West Africa, and was a thing of terrifying beauty. Tribal leaders would collect herbs, charms, amulets, and sometimes human and animal skulls, and place them in a sacred place in order to honor their ancestors and protect the tribe from evil spirits. The altar signifies a passageway between the living and dead. In voodoo, these worlds are not considered opposites, but merely different coordinates along the spectrum of ultimate reality. Candles are placed at the altar because fire represents the transformation from temporal to eternal. This recycling of energy is considered inevitable and ongoing.

The West African altar was adapted in the New World to include items from the practitioners' impoverished daily lives. Lipstick became a regular altar amulet, as did coins, tobacco, pictures of Mother Mary, and cheap bottles of whiskey and rum. The altars in Sallie Ann Glassman's shed were no exception. My eyes darted between gris-gris pouches, loose cigarettes, alligator-themed pottery, full and empty bottles of rum, crescent moons, and jewelry boxes. Necklaces, both cheap and expensive, were draped over plastic mermaids. The scene was completed by tarot cards, fresh bananas, old Raggedy Ann dolls, Christmas lights, crucifixes, unlabeled powders and herbs, perfume bottles, cosmetics, and at least one large hunting knife. It was a spectacular mess.

The doors of the shed closed behind us and the drumming resumed. Half of the group (the observers) sat on the floor near the back, and the other half (the members) danced to the beat of the drums. *Kra, ka, ka, hi. Kra, ka, ka, hi.* A torch was lit and passed. One of the members opened a bottle of Blackheart rum and took a deep drink, didn't swallow, and spit the rum into the flame, causing an instantaneous splash of fire. The ceremony was underway.

After 30 minutes of dancing, chanting, fire blowing, and singing, the members began offering small gifts—fresh fruit, cake, flowers, cigarettes, spare change—at the center altar. Soon the observers, including Andre, began leaving offerings of their own. I checked my pockets, curious to see what I could contribute, and found only my iPhone, keys, and wallet. Disappointed, I looked down and noticed the yellow wildflowers inside my jacket pocket, still fresh, that Laura had given me hours earlier. They were perfect. Holding the wildflowers as an offering, I approached the front of the room for the first time. I said a silent prayer giving thanks—to someone, anyone, whatever, but surely *something*—and placed the flowers at the altar. I felt the rhythm of the drums in my heart and my bones, and danced around the altar a few times while the congregation clapped to the beat of the drums. I returned to the back of the room with the parameters of my comfort zone expanded.

After the ceremony ended, Laura and I thanked Sallie and her friends for their hospitality. We left the shed smiling. Our unlocked bikes were waiting for us, and we rode into the distance with music in our ears.

The art of improvisation.

There is something about New Orleans that accepts, and even celebrates, the accidental. Here, a funeral is a reason to dance, and a saxophone solo is the voice of God. The spirit of New Orleans was born when brave men and women—whether slaves, musicians, or artists—broke away from the status quo and, in the quest for self-expression, discovered an unexpected logic rising from the ashes of old rules. Improvisation is an act of trusting the unknown. Trust is an act of love. Therefore, love carries us when we jump into the void and trust a safe landing. Our luck is only as good as our courage.

Magic happens   Your best self
every moment   will trust yourself
you release fear   to play the notes
and trust the flow   you do not know

Before the ceremony, New Orleans, Louisiana, 2014

CHAPTER 19

DON'T BE WEIRD

"You have to be odd to be number one."
— DR. SEUSS

igh school. Why do these two words have the power, long past graduation, to stir up such existential dread? High school, for many of us, was difficult. Not so much the classes. The classes were the easy part. The hard part was navigating the expectations of a teenage microsociety, and doing anything possible—including great leaps of effort and imagination—to not, under any circumstances, do or say anything that would constitute the unshakable label of being *weird*.

Being stigmatized as weird in high school is, from the teenage perspective, a death sentence (or at least solitary confinement). So we did our best to look like everyone else, and everyone else did their best to look like us. We were all hiding, with each other and from each other.

Who could blame us? Teenage years are sensitive. We are still in the process of growing into ourselves and discovering our place in the spectrum of social relationships. Mistakes are inevitable. These mistakes are better made in private, far from the spotlight of hallways, lunchrooms, or—god forbid—school dances. High school students, for good reason, can be nervous wrecks, afraid their own shadow will laugh if they trip and fall.

But it should have ended there. After high school, as we grow into well-adjusted adults, the crippling need for peer approval disappears, right? It should. But does it? Not really. My high school years are long gone, but the social pressure to conform to the expectations of others is as strong as ever. Everyone, it seems, both young and old, is afraid of being weird.

But this insecurity misses a basic point. Being weird, contrary to popular belief, is not necessarily a bad thing. Weirdness, in fact, is often potential strength waiting to be harnessed. When we hide our weirdness, our strength also remains hidden. Throughout history, the best and brightest among us, the great creators and innovators, have been those willing to stand out and risk being perceived as weird. When I allow you to be you, and you allow me to be me—without judgment or criticism—we give each other freedom to develop our unique brand of genius. After all, everybody is weird and nobody is.

It's okay to be weird. Here's why.

1. **There is no such thing as normal.**
   The social world is made from a spectrum of personality types. There is no right or wrong place on the spectrum, only different places. The idea that there is an objectively normal way to live is a lie perpetrated by businesses, religions, and political parties in order to control people. In truth, what is normal for me might not be normal for you, and vice-versa. When we chase the *normal*, we lose sight of the *natural*. Our normal, just like our eye color, is whatever comes naturally to each person.

2. **What you think is weird is really
your superpower.**
We all have traits—physical, intellectual, or
emotional—that make us different. The Ego says
that differences are flaws that should be hidden.
The truth is that what makes us different is our
superpower. We simply must learn to harness
the power. When we learn how to use our
weirdness, instead of hiding it, we discover our
hidden strengths. Shyness, for example, might
make you a better listener. An awkward laugh
can be endearing. Our quirks, when we master
them, become our greatest strengths.

3. **What makes you weird makes
you memorable.**
When we conform to somebody else's standards,
the results will be mediocre. Nobody pays
money to see the expected; people pay money
to see the captivating. Your true self, by its
very nature, is always captivating. People won't
remember the thing you do that everybody does.
They will remember the thing you do that only
you can do. The more different—and the more
you—the more memorable.

4. **The world is starving for authenticity.**
In a world where conformity is the easiest
option, realness is extremely valuable. Deep
down everyone wants to stand out from the
crowd, but we are afraid to go first. When you
start living as your true self, and embrace your
weirdness, you give permission to those around
you to be their true selves, and they will be
grateful. Whether or not they say it out loud,

people want to see your authentic self. We are
hungry for something real.

5. **All great art was made by weird people.**
Every creative breakthrough—artistic, political,
scientific—by definition is weird because it
introduces a solution beyond what is known
and therefore demands a new way of thinking.
Embracing your weirdness is a gift that gives
the world a new perspective and pushes culture
forward. Innovation does not happen within the
status quo. Innovation happens when outsiders
challenge the status quo with weird ideas.

6. **Resisting your weirdness
makes you dark.**
Expressing ourselves feels good. Hiding our
true selves feels bad. When we allow ourselves
to be weird, we glow. But hiding our uniqueness
makes our personalities dark because we are
resisting what comes naturally to us. Just like
a black hole results from the absence of a star,
the resistance to our unique qualities, however
weird they may be, results in a dark and inverted
projection of self. By contrast, weirdness shines.

7. **Standing out is how you find your tribe.**
People often hide their weirdness for fear of
being lonely. But it is actually conformity, not
individuality, that leads to loneliness. When
we live honestly, we discover others who align
with our weirdness. This is our tribe. When we
stand up and live according to our purpose, we
will find those who have stood up before, and

we will serve as inspiration for those who will stand up next.

8. **When you own your weirdness, the world will conform.**
   When we see ourselves as capable, others see us as capable. When we see ourselves as incapable, others see us as incapable. There is power in self-perception. When we stop fitting in and start standing out, at first we will feel uncomfortable. But when we take ownership of our actions, and move beyond the fear of criticism, the world will, to the degree of our conviction, adapt to our perception of ourselves.

CHAPTER 20

MY WAY OR
THE HIGHWAY

"Nothing burneth in hell except self-will."

— THEOLOGIA GERMANICA

When Raymond Emil Busiahn volunteered to join the U.S. Army Air Corps, it was the last thing he wanted to do. What he wanted was to farm. Happily living on 40 acres of healthy soil on the outskirts of Wood Lake, Minnesota, Ray was ready to settle down and raise crops and a family. *Besides,* he thought, *who in their right mind would go to war?* But this was 1943, and Nazi Germany was advancing quickly along the eastern front of Europe, putting the entire planet on high alert.

Ray, who was in the conflicted position of being a first generation American citizen but 100 percent ethnically German, did not believe in the effectiveness of war—not just this war, any war—to achieve peace. And yet he felt little choice in the matter. The patriotic call to arms was too acute. So he exchanged his tractor and pitchfork for a bayonet and military grade Smith & Wesson Model 10 pistol, and departed to California to meet his squadron. It was not what he wanted. Months later, entrenched in rain and gunfire on cold German battlefields, it was not what he wanted. And as winter descended in 1944, when his plane was shot down near the border of Germany and

Poland, crashing hard into a midnight black field, it was not, one would assume, what he wanted.

While a Nazi prisoner of war in Stalag Luft IV prison camp, Ray kept a small Bible in his jacket pocket. It was the only thing the German guards allowed him to keep. My mother still has it, a keepsake of the father she barely knew. Ray died in 1965. My mother was only 11. When I was a boy, my mother showed me the Bible and told me stories about my grandfather. Ray's diary notes ran along the margins of the New Testament. Some notes are prayers, others are prison observations. He took special interest in Matthew chapter 6. "Your kingdom come, your will be done, on earth as it is in heaven" was underlined. In the margin was written a single word: "Sacrifice."

The path we're afraid to take is sometimes the fastest way home.

The things we dread often give us the biggest opportunity to grow. For my grandfather, this meant fighting in World War II. He wanted to avoid the war, but his calling to serve was greater than his longing to resist. The obstacles in my life are different (thank god; I wouldn't last long in combat), but the same principles apply. The Ego has many desires—this relationship, that career, the pleasure of money, the avoidance of pain—but the things the Ego desires, while they may appear fun, are not always in our long-term interest. The Ego makes distinctions about what is good and bad, but we don't always understand what will be good and bad in the long run. When we stop chasing the Ego's desires, and say yes to the path before us, we open the door to bigger possibilities than when we insist on having our way.

We often think we need certain criteria to be met in order to be happy, but the big secret is that happiness is a state of mind independent from external circumstances.

What the Ego does not understand, I learned while stranded on Culebra, is that happiness does not have an exclusive membership. Entrance is free and the door is always open. We often think we need certain criteria to be met in order to be happy, but the big secret is that happiness is a state of mind independent from external circumstances, and therefore there is no reason to resist whatever the present moment brings. What matters is inward, not outward. Washing dishes mindfully can be just as blissful as meditation. A life of poverty and love is happier than a wealthy life conflicted by the push and pull of the mind.

Every moment is an opportunity to dissolve the Ego's illusions. The mind tries to demand specific circumstances—"I want my way"—but what we need is not always what we want. The path we're afraid to take is sometimes the fastest way home.

Between the fifth and second centuries B.C.E., an unknown author (possibly the Hindu sage Vyasa, to whom the book is often attributed) wrote the Bhagavad Gita, one of the most beloved books ever written. Originally composed in Sanskrit, the Bhagavad Gita provides a wellspring of insights that explain life through stories, philosophy, and spiritual teachings.

The narrative takes place on a battlefield in ancient India. The protagonist, Arjuna, faces a moral dilemma. His people are at war, but Arjuna—like my grandfather more than 2,000 years later—questions the value of fighting. *We should retreat and avoid this dangerous war,* he thinks. Besides, Arjuna is ethnically the same as his enemies. *Why should I fight people who are related to me?* He does not see the point. But Arjuna has luck on his side. His charioteer in battle happens to be Krishna, the supreme deity and eighth incarnation of Lord Vishnu. Going to war with Krishna is like playing basketball with Michael Jordan. It has advantages.

"Perform work in this world, Arjuna, as a man established within himself—without selfish attachments, and alike in success and defeat."

— KRISHNA, BHAGAVAD GITA

The central lesson of the Bhagavad Gita is the value of selfless action. While Arjuna's Ego wishes to avoid conflict and live a pleasurable life, Krishna explains that the purpose of life is not to attain temporary and sensual satisfaction. Pleasure, Krishna suggests, is not automatically good, and conflict is not automatically bad. There is a time and place for each. So Krishna encourages Arjuna to fight—not for personal glory, but because the battle has something important to teach him. It may not be the lesson he wants, but it is the lesson he needs.

Krishna tells Arjuna that we are called to action by something greater than ourselves. Life on earth is part of a universal choreography. We must dance our part, not in isolation, but in harmony with the whole. When we expect circumstances to unfold exactly as we desire, we will usually be disappointed. Our circumstances are not always perfect, nor are they meant to be, but we have the choice to respond perfectly to imperfection. Responding perfectly means surrendering the desire for reality to be something it is not. By releasing the need for perfection, we find peace in all things.

The story of the Bhagavad Gita takes place in a world where reality has different levels—similar to the electromagnetic light spectrum—that exist on different frequencies of consciousness. We live on the human level, but there are other levels, both above and below, happening in parallel with the human experience. Like a fractal pattern, the human world is a microcosm (from the Greek "small cosmos") that reflects the divine macrocosm ("large cosmos"). Since everything is connected, every action we take, both good and bad, has a ripple effect that extends to the dimensions above and below us. The purpose of life, the story suggests, is to choreograph our thoughts and actions (the micro) to align with the purpose and intentions of the higher levels (the macro) and, like a boat leveraging the power of wind, become one with universal flow. In other words, to live a joyful life, we must, like Arjuna, sacrifice our petty desires and trust that there is a greater purpose behind our circumstances.

The origin of the word *sacrifice* stems from the Latin *sacra* (sacred) + *facere* (to make). Whenever we sacrifice the desire of our Ego, we create a sacred exchange, and make space for a higher intelligence to guide us.

Circumstances are not always perfect, but we have the choice to respond perfectly to imperfection. Responding perfectly means surrendering the desire for reality to be something it is not. By releasing the need for perfection, we find peace in all things.

The Bhagavad Gita does not condone war. The story uses war as a metaphor for daily life. When Krishna said, "The embodied soul is eternal in existence, indestructible, and infinite, only the material body is factually perishable, therefore fight O Arjuna," he was not necessarily talking about a physical fight. He was referring to the fight of manifesting our purpose in a world that is not always supportive. Every day we encounter a new battle, a new test, and we must be bold enough to continue taking action, to continue living our truth.

We can either resist challenges or we can sacrifice our desire to resist. When we resist, our struggle increases. When we sacrifice resistance, our struggle is understood from a new perspective and is more easily solved. Our struggle is not an accident. It is a rite of passage. Sometimes we must walk through fire in order to purge our dark energy and emerge renewed.

The escape.

On February 6, 1945, nearly 8,000 Stalag Luft IV prisoners, including my grandfather, were led by German officers on what would eventually be known as the Black March. The march began during the low point of a miserable German winter and would last 86 days. The routes were long and winding to avoid the Soviet Red Army from the east. The conditions were bad, even for war. The POWs drank dirty water from ditches. Sickness ran rampant. It was not uncommon when a prisoner became ill for a German officer to pull the sick POW aside. A single gunshot was heard and the officer would return to formation alone.

Ray Busiahn survived the Black March, and returned safely to Minnesota decorated as a hero for making a valiant escape in broad daylight and taking a fellow American with him. They understood that their chances of surviving the war as Nazi prisoners were slim, so when one of the German officers was relieving himself in the ditch, Ray saw an opportunity and ran for his life. He continued running for two days deep into German terrain. Ray's co-escapee, Staff Sergeant Lowell "Slats" Slayton, was badly sick and on the verge of dying.

"I was a mess, I mean a real mess, and by now I could barely walk," Slats told William L. Smallwood in his book *Valor, Guts, and Luck.* "And I told Ray that he had to be the guide, that I couldn't even think about which direction to go. Actually, I think I was as close to dying as I have ever been. I could almost see it coming. But Ray literally saved my life. He was patient, he walked my pace, and he kept encouraging me while I stumbled through the trees."

After days of wandering the wilderness, Ray and Slats stumbled upon Russian allies cooking potatoes at a campfire.

"I realized how I had lucked out meeting Ray," Slats said. "He was German and spoke the language fluently—and these Russians, who has probably been slave laborers working for Germans for a year or more, could also speak German. Quickly, Ray explained our hunger problem and soon they were handing each of us a potato. Man, they were hot and I'm sure I burned my mouth. But I couldn't wait; I had to get that sucker in my belly, so like a hungry pig, I devoured it."

The Russians kept Ray and Slats alive, and they soon encountered British troops who led them back to allied camps where they were granted permission to return home. Ray's farm was waiting.

Grab your demon by the horns.

My grandfather's calling to battle, just like Arjuna's, was not what he wanted. His journey to prison camp in Nazi Germany, and eventually back home to Wood Lake, was filled with peril. But the moral of this story has nothing to do with war. What Ray and Arjuna learned when they reluctantly agreed to engage in battle was the value of keeping a neutral mind in the face of conflict.

"Let us not wish that things were different," they might have said. "Let us wish to accept *that which is*. Let us not wish to remove obstacles. Let us wish that they did not bother us. Let us not wish for protection. Let us wish to release fear."

Our hands are free to carry the light only when we have released attachment to personal desire. We must fight, not for ourselves, but against the selfish impulses of the Ego. Humans are driven by two opposing forces. The Bhagavad Gita calls them *daivic* and *asuric*, the godly and demonic. A modern translation might be "purpose" and "selfishness." Selfish action is a dead end, but the road opens when we fight to live our purpose.

Our farm is on the other side of the battle, and freedom is on the other side of fear. Glory comes from grabbing our demon by the horns.

PEOPLE MAY
FORGET YOUR
WORDS BUT THEY
WILL ALWAYS
REMEMBER
YOUR VIBES

CHAPTER 21

I AM LIMITLESS

F rom my office window I watched the summer sun
wake up from hibernation and descend onto Madison Avenue. Pedestrians flocked to food trucks while
birds and skirts fluttered in the breeze to brighten the
corporate shadow of midtown Manhattan. It was 3:00 P.M. on
Thursday. I looked away from the window and returned to my
computer screen, and considered opening a beer. It seemed
unfair, after all, to witness the birth of summer without a sem-
blance of celebration.

Coming from my headphones, Patti Smith's album *Horses*
hit my ears like a visionary drug, and I sat unmoving like a
soldier, although my mind, as usual, was elsewhere. Business
seemed pointless while the sun made such a remarkable trip
toward the Hudson River. *I may be stuck in the office, but
today is a good day,* I thought. *Now where is that beer?*

My idyllic mood vanished when my company's CEO
stepped into my office with the abruptness of an alarm clock.

"I'd like to see you in my office," he said.

I did not want to leave Patti Smith behind, but Patti Smith
was not paying my rent. Removing my headphones, I followed
the CEO to his office.

"James, I'm disappointed," he said, closing the door. "What
happened during last week's pitch?"

He was referring to an important presentation I had given
to a prospective client. Winning their business would have
been a huge success for our agency. Our pitch was extensive,

including website prototypes, advertising campaign ideas, and a media plan for the upcoming year.

"They decided to go with a different agency," I answered.

The CEO leaned back in his chair and looked at the ceiling. "James, I put you in charge of this pitch for a reason. I trusted you. We did not win the business, and that is okay. It happens. But I received complaints about your leadership, and that is not okay. I heard that you were not open to anyone else's ideas. You wanted to be a hero and win this business by yourself."

My body sank into my seat. He was right.

"The presentation was fine," the CEO continued. "But we failed because you had the arrogance to think you could succeed alone. Do you understand why an agency hires different departments? Because each department has strengths that support the weaknesses of other teams. Account directors build a relationship with the client. Strategists do research and make a plan. Information architects build the user experience. Designers make it look good. Developers make it work. I started this company by myself, but the reason we have grown is because I realized I didn't have all the answers. We don't need you to be a hero, James. We just need you to be part of the team."

I told the CEO that I understood and returned to my desk. Office karma is hard to earn. I had blown mine on a single hand and busted.

Nothing is more beautiful than New York City when summer finally breaks. All of Madison Avenue was basking in the afternoon outside my window, drinking iced coffee and leaving work early. But none of it mattered to me. I quietly got back to work and waited for a chance to redeem myself.

Ego inferno.

What happens when the Ego takes over completely? According to Abrahamic literature, there was once a supernatural being named Lucifer. Formerly an archangel in Heaven, Lucifer later became ruler over Hell. Lucifer (whose Hebrew name translates to "bringer of light") was once God's most powerful servant. His beauty and strength were enviable to the other angels. Even in Heaven he was considered royalty, but this was not enough to satisfy Lucifer's Ego, and his power gave way to pride.

"I am limitless," Lucifer said. "Why should I follow rules?" In a burst of unchecked Ego, Lucifer, along with the angels foolish enough to join him, staged a rebellion against Heaven. It was not even close. The rebellion was swiftly dismantled and Lucifer, along with his band of fallen angels, was banished from paradise. A new dimension called Hell was created to imprison them. In this allegory, Heaven is symbolic of living in harmony with the universe, and Hell is symbolic of the separation caused by selfish desire.

"I am limitless," the Ego says. "I don't need to listen to others." But no one, not even an archangel, can succeed alone, and Ego precedes a fall from grace.

Love your limits.

Everyone has goals and ambitions. Seeking accomplishments is human nature and, in moderation, a good thing. Yet we often encounter limitations that hold us back. Some limitations are defined by physical laws (we cannot walk through walls), some are based on social convention (I cannot own a house unless I pay for it), some are related to skill (no matter how much I practice I will never be a professional singer), and some are self-created (I will not succeed because I am afraid to try). The parameters of life, both real and imaginary, prompt an important question—which limitations should we accept and which should we try to overcome? Are limitations a sign to try harder, or are they a hint that it's time to move on?

> When we try to knock down a limitation by force, we miss the message hidden in plain sight: "Go another way."

When limitations stop us from getting what we desire, we are tempted to overcome them with force, like slamming our bodies against a locked door. Challenging limitations is healthy, but, in my experience, forcing solutions is counterproductive. When we fight limitations with force, those limitations fight back and create separation, both from others and ourselves, that hinders our progress. Limitations are more easily overcome by living in a state of flow.

Every limitation has a lesson to teach us, and we must learn the lesson before moving forward. There is an unseen wisdom in the gravity that holds us down. The timing might not be right. Maybe there is an easier way. She is not as perfect as you think she is. Or maybe you are meant to reach out for support. When we try to knock down a limitation by force, we miss the message hidden in plain sight: "Go another way."

Think of life like a video game. Every video game has rules and parameters. These rules and parameters, by defining what we can do and what we cannot do, make the game interesting. Without rules there is no game. According to ancient Eastern philosophy (such as the Rigveda which dates as far back as 1500 B.C.E.), there is a system of rules and parameters built into the game of life. The Rigveda refers to this system of rules as dharma. Dharma is the cosmic order of the universe, the force that establishes all possibilities and limitations, and defines what each individual can and cannot do.

Universal dharma defines the parameters of existence on a grand scale, and each person also has a personal dharma that defines our place in the world in relation to others. My dharma is different from your dharma. We have different strengths and different weaknesses. I can do things you cannot do, and you can do things I cannot do. Neither of us is better; we simply have different dharmas. The bumblebee cannot build a dam. The beaver cannot pollinate flowers. The spectrum of personal dharmas keeps the world in balance. We are each a single piece of the same puzzle. Our purpose is not to solve the puzzle. Our purpose is to find our place.

Work flow.

Before long I was asked to lead another pitch, this time for a Fortune 500 consumer electronics brand. If we won the business it would be our agency's largest account. The pitch was massive, and included a digital strategy, design mock-ups, and campaign ideas for the upcoming year. A million ideas were spinning inside my head. I wanted to prove to my co-workers, and to myself, that I could be a better leader than I had been during our last presentation.

It was clear from the moment I sat down at the conference room table that my team, the same team I had disappointed weeks earlier, was skeptical. I had not trusted them during our last rodeo, so they did not trust me during this one. It would be an uphill battle, not only to win the business, but to win back my team's trust. The room was tense so I decided to clear the air.

"You guys have every right to be upset with me," I said. "I messed up and allowed my Ego to get the best of me. For that, I apologize. I realize now that the work we do is bigger than me. It's bigger than any of us. We are here for one reason—to support each other. Without teamwork, there is no agency, and without an agency none of us have a job. I need you. So let's build something together. Let's have fun."

We started working together as a team, cautiously at first, by defining a list of objectives. Then the brainstorming began. Everybody put their creative thinking to work to see what innovative ideas we could pitch the client. I led the brainstorm and ensured that everybody's voice was heard. Our plan was unified and we each understood our role. Sarah, our creative director, and Ryan, our information architect, would design a website prototype. Becky, our marketing director, would develop campaign ideas, and Paul, our copywriter, would add headlines. My job was to synthesize the team's work into a compelling presentation. We would present as a team, each of us sharing our contribution to the project. If we sank, we would sink together, like the band on the *Titanic* or Chicago Cubs fans between 1908 and 2016. We crossed our fingers for a better fate.

One week (and a few long nights) later, Sarah stepped into my office.

"Your designs are amazing," I said. It was still early and the office was quiet.

"Thanks," she said. "Let's hope the client agrees."

Ryan appeared in the doorway wearing a suit and tie. It was the first time I had seen him wear a suit and tie.

"They're here," Ryan said.

I swallowed the last of my coffee and we walked into the conference room. Introductions were made, business cards were exchanged, coffee was poured. We stood under fluorescent lights and gave our presentation. Mistakes were made, including typos in the presentation (my fault). Paul fumbled his notes while reading his headlines. Sarah mispronounced the name of a best-selling product. It was not pretty, but an hour passed and we were still standing. Better yet, we had stuck together.

The client thanked us, asked a few questions, and said good-bye. They had shown little emotion during the presentation and it was impossible to gauge their reaction.

"Do you think they liked it?" I asked our CEO.

"Hard to tell," he said. "But I did."

Waiting is the hardest part. Days passed, then weeks, without hearing from the client. We gradually forgot about the pitch as we became busy with new projects. It was back to business as usual. But something in the office was different. I noticed more communication. More brainstorms. Occasional high fives. Even laughter. We still had arguments, but even our arguments were pronounced with an underlying sense of trust. Everybody was busy and time passed quickly.

It was a Monday morning in July when I received an e-mail from our CEO. "We're hiring," was the subject line. "Hi team," the e-mail said. "In order to manage our incoming workload, we will be expanding our team. Knowledge of consumer electronics required."

From across the office I heard Sarah shriek in delight. We won.

A more perfect union.

"No man is an island,
Entire of itself;
Every man is a piece of the continent,
A part of the main."

— JOHN DONNE

All wealth is built on collaboration. From hunting and gathering to the invention of currency to the birth of democracy, ours is a species of shared responsibility. Ideas can happen in isolation—especially, for some reason, in the shower—but teamwork is required to solidify the fog of ideas into the substance of reality. Alone we have limits. But together our limits expand. This is why we work. Work is where we practice forging connections with others. Every strong group of people is built upon the principle of bonding where our limits meet. Even sexual attraction is a symbol of joining what we have with what we do not have. We move beyond our limits when we trust others to lift us where our powers fall.

You are not God. I am not God. But together, bolted by the union of our limits, we become shades in God's long gradient.

CHAPTER 22

DREAMS ARE STUPID

*"Imagination is the only weapon in the war
against reality."*

— LEWIS CARROLL

We are now approaching the end of the book, and I have one small favor to ask. Set your Ego aside for one minute. Take a deep breath. Turn off your mind, relax, and float downstream. Surrender your worry and your reactionary thinking. Okay good. Now, if you would, please imagine yourself as a child. Recall one of your favorite childhood memories. Take your time. Once you have a memory, the moment most frozen in time, observe yourself within the memory. Recall the person you used to be. What did you care about? What did you dream about? Look back on how big and magical the world appeared. Notice the wonder in your eyes.

Take another deep breath. Now ask yourself—in what ways have you changed since your childhood? How have your dreams changed? We all dream, at the age of innocence, about who we want to become. We feel a siren call from somewhere beyond us—somewhere within us—but over time the sound begins to fade. Or maybe we just get used to the sound, like the roar of the ocean, and we stop listening.

Okay, now loosen your grip on your thoughts. Relax further. Move into your imagination and ask yourself another question—what did you secretly know about yourself as a child that has since been forgotten?

As a kid, my dreams were outrageous. The first thing I dreamed of becoming was a dinosaur. My top choice was a triceratops, but I would have settled for a Tyrannosaurus rex. Once I was wise enough to accept the physical impossibility of morphing into an extinct species, I set my sights on the only slightly more realistic goal of playing professional basketball. Alas. This also was not to be. My height plateaued before reaching superhuman levels and my bounce pass never quite found a rhythm.

I responded by taking the Kobe Bryant poster off my wall and replacing it with a Jack Kerouac poster. *I'll be a writer instead*, I thought, and reallocated my time practicing jump shots to practicing literary tropes. I misfired just as often, but kept practicing anyway. I would never be a dinosaur or Kobe Bryant or Jack Kerouac, but I wanted to see what kind of person I could pull from young James if I dug deep enough.

Things changed as I grew older. I did not stop dreaming—not exactly—but I did stop talking about my dreams, and gradually the fire of my passions, including writing, became sedated.

All my friends dreamed big as kids. Most kids do. But the world around me gradually changed, so I changed too. One by one, the people around me began trading their dreams for paychecks and security. We started accepting roles in the system we had once rebelled against. I looked around and witnessed a sweeping and invisible epidemic, the epidemic of conformity, spreading like a virus in high school and college, infecting the people I knew and loved. It was too difficult to swim against the current, so I broke with the wave. Without the foundation of my dreams, I drifted away at sea. We all did.

By the time I graduated college, the transformation was complete. Dreams seemed more than unrealistic. They seemed silly. Now I had something, I believed, more important than dreams. I had ambition. Eventually the Jack Kerouac poster was taken off my wall. Secretly, I still wanted to be a writer, but I rejected the possibility for fear of failure. In place of the Jack Kerouac poster I hung a painting of a seaside estate. *Now that's real inspiration*, I thought, believing success would make me happy. Deep down I knew it was not true. But what was I supposed to do? Following your dreams is hard in a world that follows the leader.

The time has come to reclaim our dreams.

Dream is not a dirty word. In spite of what those cranky cynics will tell you, being a dreamer does not mean you are lazy, out of touch, taking the path of least resistance, or afraid of old-fashioned hard work. Dreaming is not aimless wandering or living in a fantasy world. Not in the slightest. Dreaming is your promise to keep your mind's autonomy, and this takes courage.

When we dream, we see beyond the limitations of the Ego and take action toward a life worth living. Our dreams do not always turn out exactly how we plan, and that's perfectly okay. Our dreams are not a final solution, they are catalysts that drive us toward purpose and adventure, a north star to follow as we move across chaotic terrain. Our purpose in life is not written in an instruction manual. We must discover and claim it for ourselves, and dreaming is the first step. When we dream in the face of our demons, we discover they are not as strong as we had feared.

Dreaming is not aimless wandering or living in a fantasy world. Dreaming is your promise to keep your mind's autonomy, and this takes courage.

Dreaming does not require special circumstances. When stakes are high, bills are piling up, and office politics start to resemble modern warfare, that is when dreaming is more important than ever. When people around us are stressed by the demands of living, we have two choices. We can either become infected and spread the virus of stress, or we can reach within our minds and choose a different story. Our environment does not decide our mental health. Our focus decides. Reality is a mirror. Because our reality is a reflection of our thoughts and beliefs, the sustained state of our mind will, over time, create our environment. We get back the thoughts we project. Dreaming is not a fantasy. Dreaming is the mandatory first step toward the creation of a new reality.

Either follow your dreams or follow the leader.

Everyone has responsibilities. People expect things from us, including our families, our friends, our co-workers, our religion, and our government. This is mostly good. We live in a global community, and everybody depends on each other. But all too often our external responsibilities cause us to forget about our most fundamental responsibility of all—the responsibility of being true to ourselves. This is the highest calling we have.

When we are being true to ourselves, we allow our essence to leave the comfort of our inner world and reveal itself to the world. This sometimes requires us to swim against the current of popular opinion. Because we live in a world where dreams are considered silly, being true to ourselves can rub people the wrong way, especially when those people are afraid of change.

Some people will fight to protect the status quo. New ideas scare them. They will resist change because they fear uncertainty and find comfort in routine. Once upon a time they were afraid to follow their own dreams, and now they will fight to keep you from following yours. They will laugh at your purpose because they gave up their own purpose long ago. They thought it was not realistic. They were wrong.

"Dreams are stupid," the Ego says. "I have too many important obligations. I can't drop everything and do whatever I want."

"Following your dreams does not mean doing whatever you want," the Higher Self says. "It simply means that you act from the inside-out instead of reacting from the outside-in."

"My dreams are not practical. My life is comfortable and I'm afraid to change."

"All change is uncomfortable at first. But the pain of being stuck is worse. When you stay the same out of fear, the instant gratification of comfort is soon outweighed by a long-term lack of fulfillment. Life happens fast. Years will have passed before you know it. Your decisions today are small seeds that will bloom into the flower of your future. What will matter most in 10 years? Live your life based on your answer to this question."

"But my dreams are too daunting. I don't have what it takes."

"Even small changes make a huge impact. Following your dreams does not require you to evade your responsibilities, quit your job, and hop on the next one-way flight to a foreign city.

All your dreams are asking is that you change your perception of yourself. Stop seeing yourself as a victim of circumstances and start seeing your imagination as the creator of your world. Imagine a sailing ship. A small rotation of the helm will slightly change the ship's direction. At first this change will seem insignificant. But after many miles, a few degrees' difference will guide the ship in an entirely new direction."

Start living your dream now, or else . . .

There will be a time for everyone, not so far in the future, when we will look back and reflect on the life we have lived. At this point we will be closer to the end than the beginning. Our work will be finished. There will be nothing left to worry about. We will be blessed with the gift of perspective. Popular opinion will no longer matter. Insecurities will be dissolved. The Ego will resemble a dimming light. Freedom will be seen on the horizon. We will be open—just as when we were born—to any and every possibility. We will inhale and exhale more slowly, treasuring each breath.

At this point we will look back on our journey. No matter how many years have passed, it will seem like an instant. All the things that felt difficult in the moment will appear as momentary blinks in the eye of eternity. Even our deepest fears will be exposed as illusion. The only thing that will matter will be how we lived and how much we loved. Did we complete our mission? Did we discover our purpose? I believe we will look back and ask ourselves whether or not we lived according to the calling of our higher truth, and I believe our answer to this question will bring us either unspeakable joy or unspeakable regret.

You are not your job
or your income
your apartment
your looks
your education
your past
your fears
your thoughts
or what others think
about you.

You are more essential
than you have been taught.

You are creative energy
disguised as a person
and to remember this
is everything.

CULEBRA III:
THE OCEAN

The red-tailed hawk circled above me and darted across Flamenco Beach into the distance. The afternoon moved forward, and my experience was already fading into a memory. I looked down at the sand as time passed as it always does, without regard. Did you know that sand, when viewed under a microscope, does not look like sand at all, but rather resembles a robust ecosystem of tiny marine trinkets? Each seemingly boring grain of sand is, upon closer inspection, an amazing sculpture, unique as a snowflake, taking the unexpected shape of gemstones, seashells, honeycombs, and amoebas. Our eyes cannot see how sand truly looks because the human perspective is limited—in this case, based on eyesight—which distorts our reality. In some cases we are too small to see reality as it truly is, and in some cases, as with sand, we are too big. So we only see the surface of things. The sand I saw on Flamenco Beach did not look like a robust ecosystem of tiny marine trinkets. It was colored white and looked like a ghost, and I probably did too.

The hardest part about making a personal breakthrough is the nagging reminder that, in spite of all you have learned, you must still return to the same life, the same people, the same job, and the same apartment that had given shape to your previous reality. How do we reconcile a new mind with the same old circumstances? I guess the answer is that, no matter how much we evolve, circumstances do not automatically change; what changes is our ability to react to those circumstances. Just like a video game is programmed with rules and parameters, the field of external reality is programmed into the game of life. We cannot change the rules. But we can improve our skills and advance to the next level. The game of life is designed to make us the hero. We must only be brave enough to play.

The game of life is designed to make us the hero.
We must only be brave enough to play.

I stopped looking at the sand and looked at the ocean. It was deep blue. I felt a combination of relief and sadness as I realized for the first time how little control I had over my life. Just as ocean currents move in harmony with universal laws—controlled not by the will of the ocean, but by planetary relationships of which the ocean is merely a part—so too was my life part of the ebb and flow of something greater than myself. My Ego wanted control but control is an illusion. I have no control over anything except my reaction to the currents. I can choose to resist or flow with the tide. The ocean must be wise because, in spite of its splendor, it seems perfectly happy to trust the flow of the current. It has given up control yet always finds itself in the appropriate place. I stopped looking at the ocean and looked again at the sand.

And now I sit.

What is this invisible current that pushes us from pond to stream to river to ocean? Our stories are written by our response to the currents we face. These currents are unplanned but I do not think they are random. Sitting on Flamenco Beach I realized that my life had been one clumsy step after another toward some fuzzy purpose that became increasingly clear as I stumbled awkwardly forward. Nothing made sense in the moment but collectively it all made sense.

Daydreaming through day jobs and science class—*no I don't need medication, I'm just an artist*—while classmates and colleagues worked to uphold a system I did not understand. Trading those dreams for a job résumé that dried like brittle parchment, empty as paper money, lost, and could not be found again in the rubble of the crash. Fighting without honor for promotions, only to lose friends, and discovering the heavy sighs and lonely power of the corner office, where not even lunch is free. Making shadow pacts with my Ego in the smoky basement of my mind, who promised me the kingdoms of the world; I accepted in haste, without reviewing the fine print of the contract. Eating psilocybin chocolate in Central Park and seeing the door crack open for a moment, my Higher

Self speaking and fading, and nothing remaining except the subway back to Brooklyn alone. Looking at the menu in a restaurant that was the cosmos and telling the waiter that a studio apartment and marketing job would do just fine, thank you, and not thinking to order dessert. Sitting on different beaches in different years and looking into different oceans, thinking momentarily of the endless living connection from eyes to stars to ocean to toes, only to become distracted by bikinis and beach balls, and, not wishing to squander my vacation with pointless thoughts about an abstract universe, losing my train of thought and ordering another piña colada.

There was more. The prairie background of my childhood. The proverbs memorized in church. The songs of Bob Dylan. Stacks of notebooks filled with poetry for girls I would never speak to. The books my mother left around the house for me to discover like treasure maps. Triumphant summer nights with friends on rooftops listening to *Ziggy Stardust*, drunk on wine—our version of communion, or anti-communion, in the church of everything and nothing. The pain and redemption of office cubicles. Getting fired from jobs I never wanted in the first place. The one-way flight from Minneapolis to New York City. The hurricane. And now the island. Each of these moments, at the time, seemed disconnected. They appeared random. But looking back I do not think any of it was random. It was not planned, but it was not random.

And now I sit. The Atlantic Ocean had overflowed in violent duty to drop me here. That same ocean many miles south, in the silent peace of duty renewed, now opened before me with the same vastness of mind renewed. I stepped into the water. The sand on my feet dissolved and merged with the tide. *Inhale. Exhale. Inhale. Exhale.* My mental chatter washed away into the stillness of being. And far away the red hawk flew.

My notebook, July 2012

THE END

AFTERWORD

It has been said that after a war ends, the real work begins. How can two opposing sides live together once a line has been drawn? How do we move forward when wounds are still fresh? These are the questions we face whenever we elevate from one state of consciousness to another. I made it out of Culebra alive. But my work, and the implementation of the lessons I had learned, was only beginning. I left the Caribbean one month later with a plane ticket and the goodwill of friends Nick and Jolien, who opened their Fort Greene apartment to me. I am eternally grateful for their generosity.

Sh#t Your Ego Says is based on my experiences. This is what worked for me. I do not claim to have "the answers," and you should not follow my words any more than you would follow a stranger's advice. We must be diligent in questioning any truth that we did not discover through personal experience. Did my experience in Culebra clarify my purpose? Yes. Did I conquer my Ego? Maybe a little. Am I enlightened? Not even close. There is no magic bullet to a better life. Actually there is: practice. Happiness is a habit. Success is a habit. And habits require practice.

Meditation. Kundalini yoga. Conscious breathing. Selfless action. Listening. Writing. Looking at art. Time in nature. Walking. Prayer. Forgiveness. Gratitude. These are a few ways to practice living beyond the Ego. Facing my Ego on Culebra was hard, but returning to New York City and integrating my experience with "business as usual" was harder, and that is what this book is about. It is one thing to listen to your Higher Self while alone on a beach; it is another thing while running late for work on a crowded subway. We must keep moving when the road is rough. Inspiration is divine, but practice is the noblest act of all.

ABOUT THE AUTHOR

James McCrae is an award-winning strategist and author at the intersection of creativity and mindfulness, and the founder of Innerspace Foundation. He works with people and organizations around the world to unlock creative potential and turn imagination into results. His books blend literary narrative with spiritual insight to provide practical strategies to achieve meaningful success and inner purpose. An avid supporter of basketball, burritos, and yoga, James lives in New York City.

www.shityouregosays.com

Hay House Titles of Related Interest

YOU CAN HEAL YOUR LIFE, the movie,
starring Louise Hay & Friends
(available as a 1-DVD program and an expanded 2-DVD set)
Watch the trailer at: www.LouiseHayMovie.com

THE SHIFT, the movie,
starring Dr. Wayne W. Dyer
(available as a 1-DVD program and an expanded 2-DVD set)
Watch the trailer at: www.DyerMovie.com

Daily Love: Growing into Grace, by Mastin Kipp

F**k It: Do What You Love, by John C. Parkin

*The Sacred Six: A Simple, Step-by-Step Process for Focusing Your
Attention and Recovering Your Dreams,* by JB Glossinger

The Space Within: Finding Your Way Back Home, by Michael Neill

The Universe Has Your Back: Transform Fear to Faith,
by Gabrielle Bernstein

All of the above are available at your local bookstore,
or may be ordered by contacting Hay House (see next page).

We hope you enjoyed this Hay House book. If you'd like to receive our online catalog featuring additional information on Hay House books and products, or if you'd like to find out more about the Hay Foundation, please contact:

Hay House, Inc., P.O. Box 5100, Carlsbad, CA 92018-5100
(760) 431-7695 or (800) 654-5126
(760) 431-6948 (fax) or (800) 650-5115 (fax)
www.hayhouse.com® • www.hayfoundation.org

Published and distributed in Australia by: Hay House Australia Pty. Ltd., 18/36 Ralph St., Alexandria NSW 2015 • *Phone:* 612-9669-4299 *Fax:* 612-9669-4144 • www.hayhouse.com.au

Published and distributed in the United Kingdom by: Hay House UK, Ltd., Astley House, 33 Notting Hill Gate, London W11 3JQ • *Phone:* 44-20-3675-2450 • *Fax:* 44-20-3675-2451 • www.hayhouse.co.uk

Published and distributed in the Republic of South Africa by: Hay House SA (Pty), Ltd., P.O. Box 990, Witkoppen 2068 • info@hayhouse. co.za • www.hayhouse.co.za

Published in India by: Hay House Publishers India, Muskaan Complex, Plot No. 3, B-2, Vasant Kunj, New Delhi 110 070 • *Phone:* 91-11-4176-1620 • *Fax:* 91-11-4176-1630 • www.hayhouse.co.in

Distributed in Canada by: Raincoast Books, 2440 Viking Way, Richmond, B.C. V6V 1N2 • *Phone:* 1-800-663-5714 *Fax:* 1-800-565-3770 • www.raincoast.com

Take Your Soul on a Vacation

Visit www.HealYourLife.com® to regroup, recharge, and reconnect with your own magnificence. Featuring blogs, mind-body-spirit news, and life-changing wisdom from Louise Hay and friends.

Visit www.HealYourLife.com today!